CHILD SUPPORT

CHILD SUPPORT

A COMPLETE, UP-TO-DATE AUTHORITATIVE GUIDE TO COLLECTING CHILD SUPPORT

MARIANNE TAKAS

1817

HARPER & ROW, PUBLISHERS, New York
Cambridge, Philadelphia, San Francisco, London
Mexico City, São Paulo, Singapore, Sydney

To Ellen,
my sister and my friend

Grateful acknowledgment is made for permission to reprint the quote on page 121. Copyright © 1963 by Al-Anon Family Group Headquarters, Inc. Reprinted by permission of Al-Anon Family Group Headquarters, Inc.

FIRST EDITION

Designer: Jénine Holmes

Library of Congress Cataloging in Publication Data

Takas, Marianne.
  Child support.

  Includes index.
  1. Child support—Law and legislation—United States.
I. Title.
KF549.T35   1985   346.7301'72   85-42593
                         347.306172

ISBN 0-06-015475-6   85 86 87 88 89 10 9 8 7 6 5 4 3 2 1
ISBN 0-06-096021-3 (pbk.) 85 86 87 88 89 10 9 8 7 6 5 4 3 2 1

CONTENTS

Acknowledgments

My deep thanks go to Joanne Schulman, legal counsel to the National Center on Women and Family Law, and Lillian Kozak, CPA, of the NOW New York State Task Force on Domestic Relations Law. These two women gave generously of their time and experience to help refine my ideas, review my rough drafts and catch my mistakes. The first day I met Joanne, I thought I'd take her out to a leisurely lunch and perhaps pick up a few hints or ideas for the book. Instead, she took me out for a corned beef sandwich and three hours of nonstop excellent advice. As for Lillian, her exceptional intelligence is matched only by her sense of humor. This book is far richer for the help, encouragement and expert assistance of these two outstanding women.

Numerous others were also generous with their ideas and insights. Virginia Nuta of the national office of Parents Without Partners, Carol Lefcourt of the New York State Division of Women, and Emily S. Bair of the Atlanta firm of Hurt, Richardson, Garner, Todd and Codenhead were all especially helpful. Special thanks also go to the Coalition of State and Local Child Support Enforcement Organizations and to the many local parent organizers who inspired me not only with their ideas but with their energy and commitment. Finally, Diana Finch of Ellen Levine Literary Agency and Sallie Coolidge of Harper & Row, Publishers helped ease my job by doing theirs so well.

While writing this book, I was blessed with five housemates who encouraged me from the start, read rough drafts, debated ideas and never complained about my meager cooking around deadline time. Thanks therefore go to Phil Korman, Carol Hetrick, Jeb Brugmann, Claudia Cahan and especially my fellow writer and critic-of-first-resort, Alfie Kohn.

I'm told it's no longer fashionable to thank one's teachers in a book acknowledgment, but I'll just have to be out of date. Cynthia Piai Hoopes of Chagrin Falls, Ohio, taught me to take joy in reading and writing. Martin Benjamin of Michigan State University taught me about disciplined thinking and also, by example, how to really listen and learn. Teachers shape their students and then let them go, but these two sent pieces of themselves with me.

When I was a kid and the word for *activist* was "troublemaker," my family used to worry what would become of me. They were amused when I made a formal complaint to the principal of my kindergarten regarding the condition of the jungle gyms, but were a little unnerved some years later when I contacted the Equal Employment Opportunity Commission because I'd been denied work on a "boys only" golf caddy crew.

What I couldn't tell them then was that they'd always helped inspire me, even when we disagreed. From my father I learned the excitement of gathering new ideas, and from my mother the importance of commitment to a cause. For that, and for much more, I thank them.

Finally, my loving thanks go to Ed Warner, an intelligent, perceptive and supportive friend whose ideas are a constant help in shaping and refining my own. Ed's insights about family and societal relationships seem to derive both from his proud identity as a strong and loving man and from his firm conviction that a system of patriarchy oppresses us all. That perspective has certainly enriched my life—and, I hope, this book.

Preface: New Hope and New Help

"Mom, do you have two dollars? Our class is going to the Science Museum tomorrow, and we need to bring money for the bus."

It's a simple enough request, and in an ideal world it wouldn't make your heart thump. Yet if you're like many divorced or single mothers today, struggling to make ends meet, it probably does. Without adequate help from the children's father, it can take every cent of your family income just to provide for your family's most basic needs. Even a simple class field trip can be too much for an already strained budget.

If this sounds familiar, you're not alone. Today millions of families are headed by single mothers, and most experience the frustration of limited family income and lack of reliable child support. In fact, among female-headed families with children in the home, nearly two-thirds receive no child support at all,[1] and about one-third actually live below the poverty level.[2]

Yet, shockingly, the fathers of these children may live in relative comfort. One study shows that although the standard of living of women and children drops by an average 73 percent after a divorce, men's standards of living actually *increase* by an average 42 percent.[3] Another study reveals that men with incomes of $30,000 to $50,000 a year are just as likely to fail to pay court-ordered child support as are men with incomes under $10,000.[4] Not surprisingly, mothers like you and other concerned citizens are demanding more fairness and accountability.

Until recently, child support enforcement just wasn't taken seriously in our society. Support cases were given low priority by most courts and were often complicated and expensive to pursue. Even if a custodial mother persisted, the nonsupporter was generally let off with a warning (even if he'd been warned and warned before). Jailing was disfavored, and enforcement methods such as withholding support from paychecks were often either unavailable or hard to use.

By and large, in fact, men either paid voluntarily, out of a sense of responsibility and fatherly concern, or they didn't pay at all. Neither the courts nor the law enforcement agencies (nor any other public agency) were consistently helpful in collecting support.

Today the situation is improving, but widespread change doesn't happen overnight. You still need to work to make sure that promises become reality. In a very real sense, when you puruse a child support case, it's not simply a conflict between you and your child's other parent. You're really learning to take on and tackle a *system:* a legal system that's been slow to act on behalf of children, a government enforcement system that sometimes gets bogged down in red tape and a social system that often undervalues the important work of raising children.

Fortunately, you needn't struggle alone. All over the country, custodial parents have banded together to work for tougher enforcement laws and policies. In addition to their political activities, many of the groups provide emotional support and technical assistance to parents pursuing child support collection actions.

Additionally, the growing public demand for effective child support enforcement has resulted in a nationwide strengthening of the laws and programs available to help collect support. The federally sponsored Office of Child Support Enforcement, created in 1975 primarily to serve lower income families, is now mandated to assist any family needing support collection services. Recent federal legislation also requires all states to promptly improve their support enforcement laws (or risk losing federal funds).[5]

Courts, too, are finally beginning to change their policies. Get-tough practices are becoming increasingly common, and the worst offenders may even be jailed briefly or placed on probation. Some county prosecutors' offices now have entire programs devoted to using child abandonment laws to collect support. In most cases, of course, drastic remedies aren't needed, but just knowing they exist can improve overall collections dramatically.

This book is your guide to the laws and services now available to help you collect child support. It's a step-by-step handbook with a simple purpose: to demystify the legal system and help you collect support. You'll learn that while no law or program will make child support problems go away, good laws can be powerful tools. Armed with knowledge of what's available, you'll be ready to take action and make crucial decisions.

As you pursue your children's support case, you'll find that there are special factors to consider based upon your own family circumstances. You may be single (never married), married but separated, married but about to be divorced or already divorced. Your family may already have a support order, or you may be seeking one. Your children may have a good relationship with their father, a poor one or none at all.

Whatever your family situation, you'll find chapters in the book to address your concerns. Chapter 8, for example, is specifically for single mothers, while Chapter 12 is for married mothers considering a divorce or separation. As you read, feel free to skip over any chapter that you're sure doesn't apply to you. In case of doubt, though, it's a good idea to at least skim the chapter before reading further.

Here's a quick overview to help acquaint you with the book. Part One is devoted to describing and discussing the various public agencies and private professionals who can help you with support actions. We'll look at the pros and cons of the different agencies and the different kinds of support actions. Practical considerations, such as cost and efficiency, will be stressed.

In Part Two, you'll learn about how to get a child-support order that really serves your family's needs and how to avoid or solve common problems. Finding an absent parent who has secretly left town, for example, or establishing paternity if you were never married to the father, would be first priorities. For those currently or about to be involved in a divorce action, we'll look at how child support fits into the larger divorce process and how you can safeguard your family's future through a fair and comprehensive separation agreement. Protections against violence, abuse and disruptive custody switches are also discussed.

Finally, in Part Three, we'll explore the methods available to collect overdue support. You'll learn how to prove the amount that is owed, how to collect it from wages or property or other means and how to guard against defenses commonly offered by nonsupporting fathers. Most important, you'll see that you *can* establish and enforce a reliable payment habit, even if you've never collected support before.

Our children deserve the support of both parents. They deserve safe homes and decent food and warm clothing. They deserve, when the other kids go on a field trip, not to be left behind.

Establishing and collecting child support isn't always easy, but it can be done. With knowledge, pluck and persistence, you can make it possible. Child support: because your kids deserve the best that two parents can give them.

A NOTE TO CUSTODIAL FATHERS

If you're a single father reading this book, you probably have a lot of concerns in common with single mothers. You, too, may be raising a child or children without a lot of help from their other parent, and you may feel it's time to seek some financial support. It doesn't help you to know that most mothers provide most of the care for most children—all you know is that you're doing a lot for your kids and want the best for them from both parents.

This book is for you, too. All the laws and programs described here are equally available to men and women, and most custodial parents' groups welcome male membership.

In writing this book, a serious effort has been made to avoid sex stereotyping. Whenever possible, terms like *custodial parent* and *noncustodial parent* are used instead of the common *custodial mother* and *noncustodial father* (or *absent father*). You won't see references to what "men do" or "women do," though you may see common trends discussed in terms of "many women" or "many men."

At the same time, it is true that the overwhelming majority of nonsupporting parents are men and that most of the custodial parents reading this book will be women.[6] It's also simply not realistic or responsible to avoid making distinctions when discussing matters affected by widespread social, economic or biological differences between men and women in our society.

The simplest example would be the chapter on Establishing Paternity. It's both factually and legally clear that the person who gives birth to a child is that child's natural mother, so a chapter on "Establishing Paternity or Maternity" would obviously be a bit silly.

More subtly, it's hard to talk intelligently about family finances without addressing male/female differences in a society in which even full-time working women still earn only 59 cents for every dollar earned by men.[7] It's also unwise to discuss custody and support issues without recognizing the documented fact that in most families, women still provide the majority of the child care.[8] In fact, much as we'd all like to see perfect equality between the sexes, it can be unrealistic and unfair—and produce bad advice—to pretend that that equality has already arrived. For this reason, this book is not and cannot be entirely gender neutral in approach.

Unquestionably, there are many men who have important and positive relationships with their children and who support them generously and reliably. Some men have even taken on a primary parenting role. Every involved parent, male or female, deserves recognition and encouragement. This book is meant to provide, not undermine, that kind of encouragement.

As you read, then, you may have to use your imagination when language or examples don't quite fit. Women have for years read and heard phrases like, "When you go to a doctor, *he*..." and made a conscious effort to remember that a doctor can be a "she." With deepest apologies, we ask you to do the same now with any reference to a nonsupporter or noncustodial parent as "he."

I

WHERE TO
GET HELP

This book is designed to provide general information about child support; however, the publisher and author are not engaged in rendering legal or other professional services to the reader. Since individual cases do vary, the reader should consult with a competent professional on questions specific to the individual. No attorney-client relationship is created by the purchase or use of this book.

1

Taking Charge of Your Case

There are two cardinal rules to consider as you pursue your child support action. First, it's not on your shoulders alone. There are people who can assist, advise and encourage you at every step of the process. Low-cost, government-sponsored child support services are available in every state. Additionally, if you want your case handled by a private lawyer, you may be able to find one who will work for a percentage of support actually collected so you won't have to pay in advance.

On the other hand, no one will do it for you and do it right unless you're actively involved. You need to be ready to do some footwork, to assist in planning, to prod, to cajole and to make decisions. This takes energy and persistence, but it's well worth the effort. Keep in mind that a lawyer has many cases. You have one: yours. Naturally you'll be putting more energy and thought into that one important case.

Ultimately you and your children are the ones who will live with whatever financial arrangements are negotiated. It's your case, and the lawyer or child support worker who assists you works for you. This is true whether it's a lawyer you pay privately or a government service worker. You are still the client and should be entitled to make major decisions.

When you go to your first visit with any lawyer or child support worker, arrive prepared. Whether you've chosen an agency or a private lawyer, the people you talk with will need certain information about you, the noncustodial parent and the children.

To help you organize, there's a Case Information Form at the end of the book, in the appendix, with the basic information commonly needed. Fill it out as completely as possible (leave blank what you don't know), and bring it with you to your first appointment. It will speed up your case and save interview time for more in-depth planning.

As the case progresses, stay in close contact. Don't be afraid to call to ask about delays or to supply new information. The open lines of communication will help your lawyer or caseworker to stay informed about your case and will keep you from being forgotten or lost in the shuffle.

You'll work best with your lawyer or caseworker if you work cooperatively, trading ideas and information. As you read this book, you'll learn a lot about making a strong case, and you'll probably have many questions and suggestions. By all means, share them. The best lawyers learn not only from law books but from their clients as well.

If you don't get the service and commitment your case deserves, there are remedies available to you. If you've hired a private lawyer who neglects your case, you can simply take your business elsewhere. In cases of misconduct, you may wish to make a complaint through your state lawyer disciplinary board. The boards will investigate your complaint and, if necessary, take disciplinary action. You can find out about the procedures for making a complaint by contacting your state or local bar association.

If your case is being handled improperly by any of the agencies described in the book, you have other remedies. You can request a conference with the director of the local program office and follow up with a letter stating your concerns with copies to your caseworker, the department supervisor, the state agency director, and any local organizations concerned with support enforcement.

If that's not effective, you may wish to contact your state attorney general's office and your governor's office. Since states should now all have state commissions on child support enforcement that report to the governor, you may wish to make your complaint through them. State and federal elected officials (senators and members of Congress) may also be helpful. Finally, problems that appear to be widespread should be reported by certified letter to: Director, Federal Office of Child Support Enforcement, 6110 Executive Boulevard, Rockville, Maryland, 20852.

There's also a great deal that you can do in your private life to help make your case go smoothly. As much as possible, avoid unnecessary arguments with the noncustodial parent. They can only heighten any hostility and strain family relations, and they may even hurt your child support case. It's natural to be angry when you're struggling without support to raise your children, but what you really want is results. Put your energies into effective support collection and you'll be more likely to get them.

It may come as a surprise to you, but far more divorce and support cases are resolved by agreement than are ever decided by a judge. In fact, 98 percent of all divorces are settled by the parties and never go to court at all.[1] You can be sure that many of those cases started with both spouses angry and unwilling to agree, but the fact remains that a mere 2 percent actually came to trial.

In general, the key to getting results is to be fair but firm. Insist upon your rights, but treat the noncustodial parent with courtesy and respect. The more he feels respected as a parent and a family member, the less he's likely to resist paying court-ordered support. If he does resist, taking him to court to demand payment is simply being firm, and is not in the least unfair. Criticizing him in front of the children, however, would *not* be fair, and wouldn't help your case.

You should also keep in mind the importance of obeying any court orders, whether or not the noncustodial parent does his part under the order. For example, you may get an order that says the noncustodial parent must pay X dollars in child support and can have the children visit him every Saturday. If he willfully refuses to pay the support, it might be tempting to refuse to allow the children to visit him.

Don't do it. It would probably upset and confuse the children, and it could also cause you big problems in court. Legally, it is the children who have the right to child support, and the children, too, who have the right to maintain a relationship with both parents. The noncustodial parent's failure to live up to his responsibilities therefore would not justify your failing to live up to yours. A judge hearing the case might lose patience with both of you, or could even take the noncustodial parent's side in the conflict.

Of course, it's really only tempting to do something like that —to cut off the visitation in the hope of forcing support payment—when you feel powerless to collect it any other way. Fortunately, you're not. This whole book is about all the other ways available to you.

Another excellent way to feel empowered, as well as to get valuable help, information and emotional support, is to join or start a local group of custodial parents working for improved support enforcement. These groups are especially effective— and necessary—in pushing for improved agency and court performance. There are active groups all across the country, and you can check the state-by-state listing of services at the back of this book to find the group nearest you.

If there's no group listed for your area or you have trouble reaching a listed group, call the national office of Parents Without Partners toll-free at 1-800-638-8078. They maintain an up-to-date listing of new groups, as well as address and phone changes for established groups. Also, if you're interested in organizing a new group, Parents Without Partners can provide valuable help and resource information.

Taking charge of your child support case is really just one way of taking charge of your life. The practical and financial arrangements you make through the child support process will affect not only your income but also your life-style for years to come. Through your active involvement in the process, you can help guarantee that the arrangements will be workable, reliable and in tune with your family's present and future needs.

2

The Office of Child Support
Enforcement

If your family is in need of child support, you're probably looking for collection services that are comprehensive, efficient and
affordable. Many families find just that at the Office of Child
Support Enforcement (OCSE).

The OCSE is a cooperative project of local state governments
and the U.S. Department of Health and Human Services. Available in all fifty states plus the District of Columbia, Puerto Rico,
the Virgin Islands and Guam, the OCSE offers a wide variety
of enforcement services. It can help you locate a parent whose
address is unknown, establish paternity if you were single when
the child was born, get a child support order and actually collect
support. OCSE offices will also work to collect alimony, but only
if there is already a valid court order for alimony *and* child
support. They cannot assist you in getting a divorce, a property
division or an order for alimony.

Although the OCSE program has only been in operation
since 1975, it already has a respectable collection record. With
substantial strengthening and expansion of the program now
underway, its services will probably continue to improve. In
fact, it could actually be quicker and easier for you to collect
support through the OCSE than it would be if you hired a
lawyer privately.

Interestingly, the OCSE was originally conceived largely as
a way for the federal and state governments to save money on
Aid to Families with Dependent Children (AFDC). Because
government reports showed that the majority of children receiving AFDC had noncustodial fathers capable of supporting

7

them, lawmakers wanted to shift the burden of support from the government to these fathers. To accomplish this goal, Congress passed a law creating the OCSE in 1975. (You may also hear the OCSE called the IV-D Program after the law that created it, Section IV-D of the Social Security Act.)

Although the program was officially open to any family in need of support enforcement, at first the federal government encouraged state OCSE offices to focus on AFDC-related cases by offering cash incentives for collections in those cases. In recent years, however, the emphasis has changed. While the OCSE does still handle AFDC-related cases, private non–AFDC related cases now account for over half of all support collected. To help encourage these efforts, the federal government has begun paying cash incentives for non-AFDC as well as AFDC collection cases. This is important because means that your state OCSE office should be more motivated to give your case the time and attention it deserves.

The new cash incentives are only a small part of a major initiative to improve and expand the OCSE program. Under the federal Child Support Enforcement Amendments of 1984 (amending the Social Security Act), states are required to strengthen their OCSE programs promptly with approved enforcement techniques. If they don't, they risk losing federal incentive payments.

The new improved procedures now available include:

- automatic withholding of child support from paychecks
- withholding of overdue support from state and federal income tax returns
- a procedure to require nonsupporters to supply cash bonds or other security to guarantee that support will be paid
- procedures for seizing property of a nonsupporter to collect a support debt
- reporting of nonsupporters to credit agencies

Additionally, the new law requires each state to develop streamlined, or "expedited," procedures for use in OCSE child support collections. This means less use of traditional family court judges and formal judicial procedures, and use instead of quicker, more informal procedures. Generally the expedited procedings are conducted by specially trained lawyers known as administrative law judges, special masters or friends of the court. Because quick and certain action is so important in support collection cases, expedited procedures can increase effectiveness in many cases.

If your family is receiving AFDC during the time you're getting child support collection services from the OCSE, all services will be free of charge. Even if you are not receiving or eligible for AFDC, collection fees will still generally be quite low. Initially you may be charged an application fee of up to $25. In many states, however, the fee may be less, may be charged to the noncustodial parent instead of to you or may be waived or reduced for lower-income families.

Some states also charge for the actual administrative costs of a case, including staff time, court costs and (if applicable) blood test fees for paternity cases. Fortunately these costs are generally kept to a minimum and charged only if the case is successful. If necessary, the costs might be charged to the noncustodial parent or be deducted gradually out of support payments that are collected. Since charges and procedures do vary by state, you should check in advance to see what the costs will be.

HOW THE OCSE COLLECTS SUPPORT

The state OCSE offices use a variety of enforcement techniques and resources. In addition to using their own in-house remedies, they regularly cooperate with other governmental agencies and programs to bring you a comprehensive collection service.

Most cities and large towns have local OCSE offices. If there's not one listed in the phone book under state government listings, just contact the state government information number. There's also a state office listed under your state in the Resources section of this book; it can direct you to the local office nearest you.

Your collection case will start with an intake interview, where a child support worker will meet with you to gather information and assess the case. You can also use this meeting to ask any initial questions about how the case will be handled, what will be required of you and whether there will be any additional fees. To assist the worker in preparing your case, be sure to bring the completed Case Information Form from the appendix.

If you don't know where the noncustodial parent is living or working, the OCSE will help you track him down by checking with former employers, family or friends, as well as local resources such as utility companies or city directories. If that's not successful, they'll initiate a nationwide search of computer records through the federal and state Parent Locator Services (see Chapter 7).

If you're not married to the father of your child, the OCSE will prepare a form for the father to acknowledge paternity. By acknowledging paternity, the father accepts the legal responsibilities of parenthood, including the duty to support. Most fathers sign voluntarily (with or without some persuading), but if not, the OCSE can institute proceedings to prove paternity and establish the support duty (see Chapter 8).

Once the noncustodial parent is located and paternity is established, the actual child support process will begin. If you don't already have a child support order, the OCSE can help you get one. Exact procedures vary by state, but here's a general idea of how it's done.

The OCSE workers begin by contacting the noncustodial parent and advising him that he must appear for an interview. At the interview, they'll gather income information and begin bargaining for a reasonable support amount. If an agreement can't be reached, a hearing will be set up before an *administrative law judge* (ALJ) or a *special master,* who will consider the financial circumstances of both sides and decide on a support amount. Whether the support amount is set by agreement or by an ALJ's decision, it will be made into a legally binding court order. If either you or the noncustodial parent is dissatisfied, the order can be appealed to a regular family court. (See Chapter 9.)

The OCSE will also follow through to see that support orders are enforced, whether it's an old order issued by a family court or one they helped you get. That's where the improved enforcement laws are important. Probably the tool that will be used most often is *wage assignment,* which can be imposed if support payments are even one month late. Once a wage assignment is operating, the noncustodial parent's employer will deduct support payments from his wages and send them directly to you or to the OCSE office. If a wage assignment isn't practical, one or more other enforcement methods will be used.

At times, the OCSE makes use of the services of other enforcement programs, either by referring cases or working cooperatively with the other program. Each of the programs described in Chapters 3 and 4 commonly have cooperative arrangements with the OCSE.

GETTING THE SERVICES YOU NEED

The OCSE is a huge public agency, and, as in any large agency, cases can get lost in the shuffle. Some state offices perform better than others, and within a given office, some workers perform better than others. In general, OCSE performance has been reasonably good, but it still makes sense for you to keep out a watchful eye.

The important point is that the tools are there to collect support effectively. The OCSE services are potentially excellent, and you have a right to receive them. If all goes well, you may collect support promptly and reliably, without a need for constant action on your part. If not, it's up to you to insist on the services your family needs and deserves.

If there is a problem with your case, you might seek the help of a local parents' group (or organize one if there isn't one already). A good custodial parents' group can do a great deal to help improve local OCSE performance, particularly if it can work out a cooperative relationship with the agency.

Your group could, for example, request a meeting with local OCSE administrators, emphasizing the shared concern for effective child support enforcement. In the meeting, you might ask how your group could help the OCSE efforts, perhaps by offering encouragement to custodial parents seeking support through the OCSE, or more tangible aid such as offering child care during child support hearings. At the same time, you could voice your concerns about OCSE performance, with suggestions for improvement if possible.

Quite likely your willingness to recognize and assist the OCSE efforts will make them equally willing to help you. At a minimum, they'll know who you are and be unlikely to forget your case. Either way, the result will probably be more effective enforcement efforts.

If you're currently unemployed or have a low income, you may want to consider applying for Aid to Families with Dependent Children (AFDC) to tide you over while you seek child support and/or a new job. It can give you a small monthly check, good medical coverage from Medicaid and free child support collection services from the OCSE.

Some women find it discouraging to apply for AFDC, largely due to all the prejudices and misunderstandings about AFDC recipients today. For example, many people think that once you get an AFDC check you'll never stop depending on it, when, in fact, more than half of all AFDC cases remain open for less than a year. It's also commonly believed that AFDC payments are creating a significant drain on the taxpayers, but the truth is that they represent only about 1 percent of the federal budget.[1]

However you feel about AFDC as a long-range proposition, it can be a good short-term help in getting you back on your feet again—particularly if combined with efforts to collect child support. If it helps you feel more energized, you could set a goal for yourself. You could, for example, aim to have another source of family income within about a year.

The rest of this chapter describes how receipt of AFDC can affect OCSE support collection services. If your family has never received AFDC and doesn't expect to in the future, you can skip over it. If you used to receive AFDC, receive it now or are considering applying, read on.

HOW RECEIPT OF AFDC CAN
AFFECT SUPPORT COLLECTION

When a family is receiving an AFDC check larger than the amount of child support being collected, much of that monthly support money goes to repay the government for the family's monthly AFDC check. For example, suppose your family is receiving $300 a month from AFDC, and the OCSE succeeds in collecting $200 a month child support from the noncustodial parent. Under current rules, you would continue to receive the $300 monthly AFDC check, plus the first $50 of child support collected each month. You would thus receive a total of $350 a month, plus Medicaid coverage, and would not be charged for the child support collection services.

Now suppose you were receiving that same $300 monthly AFDC check, but OCSE began collecting an amount of child support for you equal to or greater than $350 (the amount of the AFDC check plus the first $50 of monthly support). In that case, you would stop receiving the AFDC check and would get the child support instead. However, your family would continue to have Medicaid coverage for an additional four months. Also, the OCSE would continue to collect the child support for you without charging the $25 non-AFDC application fee; neither would they charge you for any of the work they'd already put into the case.

In general, the system works fairly well, but problems can arise. In some cases, for example, OCSE workers will try to negotiate a child support amount just slightly under the family's AFDC check. They may reason that it will help the family by keeping them eligible for Medicaid. It will also help the OCSE program look good, because money will be going to the government to repay the AFDC program each month.

Unfortunately, since AFDC checks are so low, this policy can result in an artificially low child support amount. If your children's father has a high or even a moderate income, you'd want to seek a child support amount that would help equalize your standard of living, not leave you on AFDC at the edge of poverty. Keep in mind, too, that if you agreed to a low support amount to stay on Medicaid, you might soon thereafter get a new job and leave the AFDC rolls anyway. You would still, however, be stuck with the low support amount.

To avoid this problem, you could ask whether this is a common practice in your local OCSE office and insist on a reasonable support level in your case. If you have questions about what's reasonable, you might want to check with a local lawyer for a second opinion.

A different problem might come up if (1) you used to receive AFDC but no longer do, and (2) you have an old order for child support and think you can finally collect on it. Under the law, you would be entitled to all present and future support due under the original support order. For example, if the order said the noncustodial parent should pay $200 a month, you'd be entitled to $200 this month and every future month the order is in effect.

You'd also be entitled to overdue back support under the order—but only for those months you weren't receiving AFDC. For the months you were receiving AFDC, the state, not you, would be entitled to seek the back support. If the noncustodial parent was also ordered to pay medical expenses, the state could seek repayment for money spent on medical care for your children under Medicaid.

Now you could quite lawfully go to court (using a private lawyer rather than an OCSE lawyer) and seek both the ongoing support and any past support owed to you and the children. You would not be entitled to collect support for any months you were receiving AFDC, but it wouldn't be your job to collect the money owed to the state for those months either. In effect, your child support case would simply ignore the months you received AFDC and would seek only the money owed to you and the children.

If you asked the OCSE to handle your case, however, they would almost certainly seek to collect money to repay the state as well as money for you and the children. Assuming the noncustodial parent doesn't have unlimited funds, this could mean less money to your family. Although the OCSE would not be allowed to collect money for the government without first seeking your $200 a month, they might not seek past support for you. They would also be unlikely to seek a support increase for you (even if the noncustodial parent's income had greatly increased over the years), because an increase to you might mean less support repaid to the government.

For this reason, it's often better to seek collection services from a private lawyer rather than from the OCSE if you have an old unpaid child support order and you received AFDC in the past for several months or more. If possible, you should at least check with a private lawyer who is experienced in child support enforcement before taking your case to the OCSE. Be sure to bring with you the original support order and to write down in advance what months you received AFDC. If there were large medical bills paid by Medicaid, also mention those bills and bring records if possible.

The OCSE services may not be right for every family, but they are right for many. Certainly, they are economical and increasingly efficient support collection services. As such, they're well worth considering.

3

Collecting Across State Lines

Until recently, leaving the state was an almost foolproof way for a noncustodial parent to avoid a support obligation. Anytime two parents lived in different states, the custodial parent trying to collect support was faced with a real catch-22. The courts in her own state could not help her, she was told, because they had no power over the noncustodial parent, who was neither a resident of the state nor present before the court. Yet with funds already limited by the lack of support, few custodial parents could afford to travel to the noncustodial parent's state to begin collection efforts.

Over the past several years, all this has changed—at first only on paper, but more recently in actual practice. Today there are several different ways to solve the out-of-state nonsupporter problem without leaving your own state. Each one takes a little more effort and diligence than an in-state case would, but all are workable in a proper case. Once you know the options, you can decide which one is right for you.

THE URESA PROGRAM

One increasingly popular way to collect support out of state is through the Uniform Reciprocal Enforcement of Support Act (URESA, pronounced your-EE-sa) program. Available in all fifty states and the U.S. territories, URESA services are generally offered free of charge to the custodial parent,[1] without any need to hire an outside lawyer. These services are available to the state OCSE offices described in Chapter 2 and also to private individuals not receiving OCSE services.

The URESA program is not actually an agency as the OCSE is. Instead, it's more accurately described as a *process*—a set of laws that every state has passed and uses to cooperate with other states in collecting support across state lines.

While every state has offices that handle URESA cases, the names and locations of the offices vary by state. (To avoid confusion, we'll use the phrase "the URESA office," but in your state it could actually be part of a larger agency such as the district attorney or county prosecutor's office.) To find the URESA office nearest you, you could call your local OCSE office and ask the staff there. You could also contact the URESA information agent listed for your state at the back of this book.

Here's how the URESA process works. Basically it is a two-court process for establishing and enforcing a child support order. You make your request for child support in your own state, and the noncustodial parent presents any defenses in his own state.

To start a URESA action, simply go to your local URESA office, bringing with you your Case Information Form from the appendix. At the office, you'll be assisted in filling out a simple form called a petition, which explains that you and the noncustodial parent are the parents of a child or children in need of support, describes your own and the noncustodial parent's financial circumstances as accurately as possible and requests a specific amount of child support.

As with any other child support action, you'll need to supply a current address for the noncustodial parent if the case is to go forward. Although technically the URESA system is supposed to help you find the address if you don't have it, as a practical matter, they really don't have the resources to do so. For this reason, you should try to get the address first before filling out the URESA petition. (See Chapter 7 if this is a problem.)

Once the petition is complete, you'll be asked to swear or affirm that the information you supplied in it is true. The completed petition is then taken to a local judge, who looks it over, makes sure it is in order and then passes it on.

From there, the case is largely handled by the URESA office in the noncustodial parent's state. Your local office will become involved only if more information is needed or if there's a problem with the case. Be sure to ask your local worker for the name and address of the out-of-state URESA office handling your case, in case you need to contact it later.

Once the case is transferred to the noncustodial parent's state, a lawyer will be assigned to represent you. The information from your petition (and any supporting information or documents you send along) will be used to prepare your case, so you can see it's important that they be as complete and accurate as possible. In fact, you'll probably never even talk directly with the lawyer handling your case.

In many ways, the URESA process in the noncustodial parent's state will be similar to any other child support proceeding. The noncustodial parent will be personally delivered a copy of your petition, thus giving the court power over him. If the noncustodial parent agrees to pay the requested support—or a smaller amount the lawyer representing you believes is reasonable—an agreement will be signed.

If no agreement is reached, a hearing will be set before a judge. Your lawyer will present your case, and the noncustodial parent will be allowed to present any defenses, with or without a lawyer's help. At the conclusion of the hearing, the judge will decide whether and how much support should be paid.

Despite the similarities between URESA cases and other kinds of support actions, there are some important differences. Because you're not there to help plan and present it, your case may suffer. Your lawyer has neither the benefit of your ideas nor the energizing sense of working with and for a concerned client. Even more crucial, the judge will meet the noncustodial parent personally and hear his concerns about tight finances, business problems and so on, but will never actually see you or the children. It's only natural that the judge may be more likely to sympathize with the noncustodial parent. Unfortunately this can cost you support dollars when the final decision is made.

Another problem with URESA is that it is often not suitable for even mildly complicated cases. Discovery, the legal process for finding out information about the other party in a case, is quite limited in most states. For example, the noncustodial parent's earnings are generally proved in URESA cases by requesting him to bring in pay stubs covering the past few months. This might be fine if the noncustodial parent's only earnings are from a steady salary, but the process could be inadequate if he had other income, a personal expense account or even separate overtime pay (see Chapter 11).

Similarly, disputed paternity cases can sometimes be a problem. Some URESA offices won't handle them, while others handle them but have a low success rate. This is, at least in part, because of the difficulty of carrying on the case without you present. Yet some URESA offices, using sophisticated blood tests and aggressive case management, are quite successful in getting paternity determinations. You can probably find out from your local URESA office how effective the out-of-state office usually is in these cases.

Finally, you should be aware that URESA actions are almost always very slow, due in part to outdated laws and/or underfunded programs in many states. According to an advisory panel for the URESA system, ninety days is considered a reasonable time for the noncustodial parent's state to wait before taking any action.[2] Some states report that an average of six months or even a year is needed before the first support payment can be expected.[3]

IMPROVING URESA PERFORMANCE

Fortunately there are several steps you can take to help improve URESA performance. One possible route is to pursue your URESA case through the OCSE. In some states, OCSE offices have more funding and better contact with out-of-state offices. To find out if this procedure is available and recommended, ask at both the local URESA office and the OCSE office.

Another possibility is to use a support order you already have (perhaps from a divorce) and seek enforcement of that order through the URESA process. You may be able to use that order as evidence of a proper support amount or, through a process called *registration,* in place of a support hearing in the noncustodial parent's state. Either way, it speeds up the process and helps avoid any reduction in your support amount. Most states that allow registration of a child support order will also enforce alimony provisions in the order.

If you have specific complaints or problems with your case, there is an office you can contact. To find it, look in the Resources list at the back of the book under the noncustodial parent's state for the Interstate Inquiries and Complaints office.

If you still have energy left over, by all means use it. The URESA system can stand a lot of improvement, and you can help through political organizing with other custodial parents. You could push for increased funding or modernized laws in your own state, or for more federal involvement to make the program work better nationwide. Your efforts could make a difference long after your own case is resolved and your children are grown.

Many states have outdated URESA laws, and political action is needed to change this. The first URESA laws were based on a model law approved by a special Conference of Commissioners on Uniform State Laws in 1950. Substantial amendments to the law were later recommended by the conference in 1958 and again in 1968, but many states have failed to adopt the amendments.

In fact, a recent analysis of URESA statutes around the country shows that New York and Iowa have interstate support enforcement laws that don't conform to *any* version of the model URESA law. Alabama, Alaska, Connecticut, Delaware, Georgia, Hawaii, Massachusetts, Michigan, Mississippi, Tennessee and Washington have all failed to adopt the recommended

URESA amendments from 1958 or from 1968. Idaho, Oregon, South Carolina, Texas, Utah and Wyoming also have failed to pass the 1968 amendments.[4]

As a result, the URESA system tends to be a rather confusing hodgepodge of differing laws and uneven enforcement. Some states allow registration of existing support orders, while others don't. A few states will take a URESA case only if there is already a support order in effect. Some but not all states process paternity actions. Most states make their services available whether or not the parents were ever married, but a few require a copy of a marriage certificate to be filed with the petition. For every important URESA provision, it seems, there are exceptions in one or many states.

Some of the resulting confusion can be resolved by reference to an interstate referral guide, distributed to each URESA office, which tells what services are available in each state.[5] If you have questions about what services you can expect from the noncustodial parent's state, ask the worker assigned to your case in your local URESA office. You might also ask whether your local office has generally found the office in the noncustodial parent's state to be helpful and effective in collecting support.

Basically the advantages of using URESA to collect support are that it is free or very inexpensive and does not require you to leave your own state. Because performance varies so greatly from state to state, you'll need to ask questions about what to expect and to show some assertiveness in following through if things go wrong. If your case is a complicated one, particularly if it involves a high-income noncustodial parent or a paternity dispute, you may want to consult a private lawyer before proceeding with a URESA case.

ENFORCING AN ORDER FROM YOUR STATE

If you already have a support order from your state, there may be a way to have it enforced directly in the noncustodial parent's state without using the URESA system at all. This method is based on the general theory of law that a valid judgment of any state court is entitled to "full faith and credit" by the courts of other states. In other words, the other states must respect and, if possible, enforce the judgment. This method, where practical, applies equally to alimony and child support cases.

To take advantage of this method, the first step is to request the court that issued the original support order to issue a formal judgment that the noncustodial parent now owes a specific amount of back child support. This is called *reducing the order to a judgment*. Unfortunately, not all states will allow their courts to do this without the noncustodial parent there. Where it's allowed, however, it's generally not difficult to get done. It's important because it prevents a judge in the noncustodial parent's state from *forgiving* (excusing the obligation to pay) past unpaid support.

Once the order is reduced to a judgment, you can seek collection of the amount owed in the noncustodial parent's state. You'll need a lawyer to represent you in that state, but you probably won't have to go there yourself. If you're working through the OCSE, it will use its lawyers in that state. If you're pursuing your case privately, your local lawyer will probably arrange to work cooperatively with a lawyer in the noncustodial parent's state.

Successful collection of back support will often encourage a noncustodial parent to resume paying support under the original support order. This is because it emphasizes that you are serious about collecting support and shows that the noncustodial parent is not beyond the reach of the law.

Your lawyer may also be able to have your order for continuing support *domesticated* in the noncustodial parent's state. This means that the courts of the noncustodial parent's state will adopt and enforce the order as if it were their own.

Once again, however, this method sometimes works better on paper than in actual practice. Unfortunately if you're not there to see that things get done, they may not get done right. Out-of-state enforcement through the "full faith and credit" procedures can be done but may take effort and persistence on your part.

To find out whether this method is available and practical in your case, contact a private lawyer or an OCSE lawyer.

BRINGING THE NONCUSTODIAL PARENT TO YOUR COURT

You've just learned about ways you can take a case to the noncustodial parent's state while physically staying at home. There are also ways to make the noncustodial parent come to the courts in your state to resolve his support obligations. This can be an advantage, because you'll be right there to help make the strongest possible case.

To understand how the various methods work, it's helpful to understand what gives a court personal *jurisdiction*, or legal power, over the people in a lawsuit. When you file a petition in your child support, divorce or paternity case, you automatically agree that the court will have jurisdiction over you. In a simple case, the court then gets jurisdiction over the noncustodial parent by having certain court papers personally *served*, or delivered, to him (see Chapter 9). The noncustodial parent need not be a resident of the state but must only be present within the state.

This means that if the noncustodial parent sometimes visits within the state, quick action on your part could result in his being served with the court papers before he leaves town. After that, he will be subject to the court's jurisdiction and will have to abide by all rulings. If he wants to defend his case, he'll have to appear before the court in your state.

If you think this is a possibility in your case, check with either a private lawyer or an OCSE lawyer. Specific rules on how to serve someone with a lawsuit vary by state, so you'll need advice and help. However, avoid any lawyer who suggests tricking the noncustodial parent into coming into the state (for example, by claiming there's been a family emergency). Tactics like that, in addition to being dishonest, don't work. The court will probably consider the method fraudulent and won't take jurisdiction.

LONG-ARM STATUTES

Another way a court can get personal jurisdiction over a non-resident is through the use of special laws designed to allow the "long arm of the law" to extend its power from one state to the residents of another state. Known as *long-arm statutes,* these laws are not available or practical in every state. Where they are available, however, they can allow a court to take jurisdiction even when the noncustodial parent doesn't live in and no longer visits the state.

Long-arm statutes are based upon the legal theory that any person who has even "minimum contacts" with people within a state, and through those contacts develops a legal obligation, should be subject to the courts of that state to resolve the obligation. For example, if you caused an auto accident in California, you could be sued for it in California under their long-arm statute even if you left the state before being served with the lawsuit.

By the same token, if you and the noncustodial parent had sex and conceived a child in your state, a state long-arm statute would allow you to sue for child support in your state. You would simply have to follow the guidelines in the statute for formally notifying the noncustodial parent of the support action. He would then be under the court's jurisdiction, would have to come to your state to offer any defenses and would be bound by the court's decisions.

Long-arm statutes are used by both private lawyers and OCSE lawyers pursuing paternity and/or support cases. To find out if there is one that could be used in your case, you can check with either.

EXTRADITION

A last resort for bringing a noncustodial parent to your state for a support case is through criminal extradition. This means that the noncustodial parent would have to be charged with a crime such as child abandonment in your state, arrested in his state and transported to your state. He would then be subject to criminal prosecution in your state for the crime charged (see Chapter 4).

This is obviously an extreme method not suitable for the average case. In many cases, sudden arrest and removal from the state could cause the noncustodial parent to lose his job and only source of income. It could also frighten children to know their father had been arrested as well as harm whatever family ties still exist.

Occasionally, however, extradition—or the threat of it—is appropriate when all other efforts have failed. A wealthy self-employed businessman flagrantly neglecting his children, for example, would probably come up with support money quite quickly to avoid being shipped to an out-of-state jail.

If you want to know more about the possibility of using criminal extradition in your case, contact the county prosecutor or district attorney's office in your county.

4

Tough Remedies for Tough Cases

In many states, the willful failure to support one's child is not only a private offense; it is a crime. If the crime is proved, the nonsupporter can go to jail.[1]

Common sense tells us, of course, that an absent parent who is in jail for a long period of time is not only unlikely to provide support but, unless he is engaged in a work-release program or receiving other income, is probably unable to do so. Worse yet, long-term jailing can have negative effects on the whole family. Any family ties that existed before the imprisonment may be replaced by anger and bitterness. Children may feel anxious and even guilty, reasoning that "Daddy wouldn't be in jail if it weren't for me." The noncustodial parent, once out of jail, will have a criminal record and an interrupted work record. He will probably have lost any job he held before the jailing and may have trouble finding a new one. He may even decide to flee the state, hoping to leave his troubles—and his support responsibilities—behind him.[2]

WHY CRIMINAL ENFORCEMENT CAN BE SO EFFECTIVE

Despite the hazards of long-term jailing, a fair and efficient enforcement program with a realistic threat of *short-term* jailing can, when used properly, be an effective and reasonable means of collecting support. In some cases, it may be the only method that works. It is also possible to use it in a way that does not cause undue family disruption. Indeed, in a well-managed program of criminal support enforcement, most absent parents will pay reliably, and comparatively few will spend even a weekend in jail.[3]

This makes sense when you consider that criminal penalties in general are one way that we as a society emphasize what we don't allow people to do. By placing criminal penalties on certain kinds of behavior, we express our hope and belief that most people won't behave in those ways. And, by and large, they don't.

For example, we all at times want things we can't afford to buy. If we didn't agree that it was wrong, shoplifting might seem like a tempting, even an appealing way to get them. Rarely, of course, do we walk through stores thinking, "I'd steal that but I might go to jail for it." Instead, we accept that stealing is wrong, pay our money for what we can afford and go on about our business.

Yet if no one were ever jailed for shoplifting—if there were no criminal laws against it, and shopkeepers could seek only to have stolen merchandise returned—our thinking might slowly begin to change. We might reason that shoplifting wasn't considered a serious matter by the public and the lawmakers, and we might begin to rationalize taking what we wanted. "The shopkeeper doesn't really need this dress. There are dozens just like it on the rack. I'll just take this one, and no one will know the difference."

By the same token, the noncustodial parent who knows that withholding child support won't result in any serious action may also be tempted to make excuses. "She won't spend the money on the kids anyway. Let her new boyfriend take care of them if she likes him so much. I've got to think of my own expenses."

This general theory of law and behavior is well recognized throughout our entire legal system. Even in *civil* (noncriminal) cases of all types, there is a way that judges can send people to jail if they purposely disobey court orders. Most of the time, the power doesn't have to be used; just knowing it's there makes people obey. This method, called *contempt of court*, is sometimes used in child support cases (see Chapter 17).

If jailing is a possibility in civil cases, why do some states see a need for separate criminal laws to enforce child support? There are several reasons. Often the family court judges who handle civil child support cases just don't think in terms of jailing. They're used to handling cases by compromise, not by power tactics. A criminal action may also be fairer to the non-custodial parent than a jailing for civil contempt, because he'll have certain rights protected (such as the right to have a lawyer appointed if he can't afford to hire one, the right to bring in witnesses and so on). Finally, it may be easier and more efficient to monitor.

WHEN IS CRIMINAL NONSUPPORT ACTION APPROPRIATE?

In some states, prosecutors handling nonsupport cases tend to seek criminal remedies mostly against poor and minority men, irregularly employed men and men with drinking problems or past arrest records. Men with professional or managerial positions are the *least* likely ever to find themselves threatened with jail, even if they owe just as much child support as the others.[4]

Ironically, these professional men are often the ones who are quite able to support their children but who choose not to do so. They are also far more likely than lower-income men to respond to a brief jailing or the threat of jailing with prompt and reliable payment of both past-due and continuing support.[5] For one thing, they generally have a greater ability to pay large amounts of back support than lower-income men do. They also tend (with some exceptions) to be more established in the community, making fleeing the state a less desirable option. Even if they do leave the state, they'll probably be easier to find again (See Chapter 7).

A professional may also feel he has more to lose from a criminal action than an unemployed person will. Certainly his social and professional status could suffer, particularly if his work is badly disrupted. Indeed, if the mere idea of a criminal charge being filed doesn't send him reaching for his wallet, a night or two in jail surely will. In fact, some specialists in the field have been inspired to describe criminal nonsupport actions as the great overlooked remedy for upper- and upper-middle-income nonsupporters.

Of course, a noncustodial parent doesn't have to be driving a Mercedes to be shirking his duties to his children; neither are all nonsupporting professionals callously ignoring their children's needs. The real question is willfulness. If your children's father has a good relationship with the kids and really does have some financial problems (even if exaggerated), you may feel the criminal process is too harsh a remedy. But if he truly seems to have turned his back on his children, a criminal nonsupport action might be a way to insist on at least financial involvement.

In sum, a criminal nonsupport action generally makes sense only when both of the following conditions are met:

1. The noncustodial parent appears to be willfully withholding support despite an ability to pay.
2. Civil enforcement remedies have been tried and have failed.

In such a case, criminal enforcement is certainly reasonable. If a good program is available locally, it may also be the most effective choice you can make.

HOW THE CRIMINAL ENFORCEMENT PROCESS WORKS

Criminal nonsupport laws, known in some states as *child abandonment laws,* are generally categorized as *misdemeanors.* This means that they carry less severe penalties and, for most people, less social stigma than more serious *felony* crimes, such as armed robbery or rape.

Details of the various laws and programs may vary, but here is a general description of how a good program works. Generally, criminal nonsupport cases are prosecuted through county prosecutors' offices (either by workers handling all kinds of misdemeanor cases or by ones specializing in nonsupport cases). Many but not all of these prosecutors are lawyers.

In a typical case, the office becomes aware of a nonsupport case either by referral from a family court or state OCSE, or when a parent like you comes in to request help. As in civil child support cases, the workers gather case information, then contact the noncustodial parent to request him to appear for an interview. Unless there is strong reason to believe that the noncustodial parent will try to flee, he won't be arrested to force an appearance.

Most noncustodial parents, even those who might ignore requests from a civil (noncriminal) enforcement agency, will come in or call when requested to do so by a prosecutor's office. Particularly if the program has a reputation for following through on its cases, a typical noncustodial parent will want to stay on the prosecutor's good side. Often, the parent will agree immediately to a payment plan of support owed or, if there's no support order in effect, to an ongoing support amount to be paid. If he gets the sense that it's pay up or face criminal charges, he'll probably continue to pay (at least well enough to avoid the criminal action).

If the noncustodial parent persistently fails to pay, even in response to warnings, a criminal action may result. You, as the custodial parent, would not be the petitioner in any action. The state would be the *plaintiff*, with the nonsupporter named as the *defendant*. This is because the noncustodial parent's actions are considered an offense against the laws of the state. You would also not be charged any fees during any part of the process.

There are several steps to a criminal action. They include:

- indictment (the formal written accusation of a crime)
- arrest (usually promptly followed by release upon payment of a bond)

- pretrial hearing (when the defendant is advised in court of the charge against him and of his legal rights)
- preparation of evidence
- trial
- sentencing
- appeal

In most cases, however, there's no need to go through the entire process. In a good criminal enforcement program, the noncustodial parent will be able to stop the criminal action from going forward by paying the support owed at any time. Not surprisingly, this is for most people a strong motivation to pay.

Even if there is a conviction for criminal nonsupport, it still may not result in an actual stay in jail. A common sentence in a nonsupport case is one year in jail, *probated* upon the condition that the noncustodial parent pays the support due each month. This means that the noncustodial parent won't go to jail as long as he keeps paying—but will be quickly sent to jail, with only a brief hearing necessary, anytime he stops paying without a very good reason. Since there will be a probation officer assigned to follow the case, the chances are good that any nonpayment will in fact result in quick court action. You, of course, would also notify the probation officer in case of nonpayment.

What we've described here, of course, is an enlightened and efficient criminal nonsupport program. Unfortunately, not all programs are this good. Some are inefficient, letting noncustodial parents slip by with poor payment records for years, then leaping suddenly and unexpectedly into action. Other programs may jail offenders so rarely, even in the most blatant cases, that they become known as paper tigers—all threat and no action. Still others seem to stress jailing, and even jailing for terms as long as a year, as an end in itself instead of as a means to induce reliable payment.

For this reason, it's important to ask questions about the attitudes and performance record of any criminal nonsupport office before putting your case into its hands. Ask about policies for monitoring cases, standard procedure in the case of nonpayment and overall collection rates. If possible, double check by asking other custodial parents what their experiences have been.

Keep in mind that the most important quality of an effective program is not that severe punishment is sought against nonsupporters but that enforcement is prompt, even-handed, and predictable.[6] Such a program is likely to inspire respect—*and* reliable support payment.

5

When an Independent Lawyer Is Needed

Some people think of the legal process as almost a secret world —obscure, mysterious and accessible only to those who hire a private attorney. And some attorneys, if the truth be told, seem to encourage such a view.

All of which is, of course, nonsense. You've already seen that there is a great deal you can do to help prepare your child support case, and that there are no less than three publicly available routes (the OCSE, URESA and the criminal justice system) for pursuing it. In many cases, these agency remedies may be quicker and more efficient—as well as less expensive— than hiring a lawyer on your own.

Yet it's possible that you'll have specialized needs that an agency will not be able to meet, or that your case may be complicated enough to require more individual attention. If so, you might consider using an independent lawyer.

We'll use the terms *independent lawyer* and *private lawyer* here to include not only ones you hire but also lawyers available free to low-income families through the Legal Services Corporation. This is because lawyers you hire through the private market and Legal Service lawyers have in common the fact that *you* are their primary client, not an agency or the state.

There are several types of cases involving child support that are best handled by an independent lawyer. We'll look first at those in which it's crucial to have your own lawyer, then at those in which it can be helpful.

DIVORCE CASES

Neither the OCSE, URESA or the criminal justice system can assist you in getting a divorce, dividing property and debts or negotiating alimony. Yet divorce is a process with serious practical and financial consequences, and you need good legal assistance to protect your family security.

If you've heard of do-it-yourself divorce kits or other self-help remedies for divorcing couples, you may wonder if a lawyer is really necessary. The answer is yes, for the following reason: a kit can show you how to type the legal forms you need to get a divorce as well as tell you where to go and what to do at the courthouse. For a childless couple with little property to divide and neither spouse in need of support, this might be sufficient. But with children to consider, you'll need to make serious decisions about custody, visitation, support, property division and other family matters. Each decision has important legal consequences that you should understand clearly, and a lawyer can help by explaining and advising. You may also need help negotiating and writing an agreement that is fair, clear and enforceable. For your family's welfare, a lawyer is important.

CUSTODY CASES

Another situation in which it's essential to have your own lawyer is any case involving a custody conflict. Of course, since custody cases most often arise in divorce cases, you'd probably already have your own lawyer, who would also handle the custody aspect. Occasionally, however, there will be a custody dispute between parents who've never been married. Somewhat more commonly, a custody conflict may arise between divorced parents years after the divorce, as a change of custody case.

For example, you could be pursuing a simple support collection case through the OCSE. The noncustodial parent, either out of a desire to avoid paying support or out of a true desire to see more of the children, could counterclaim (file a request of his own) for change of custody. Suddenly the case would be changed from a simple support collection case to a custody and support case. At that point, it would be wise to consult an independent lawyer with experience in custody cases.

Possibly, of course, the OCSE lawyer handling your case would be willing and able to handle the custody part, too. Unfortunately, it's not safe to assume that automatically. An OCSE lawyer is not hired to handle custody cases and may or may not have experience with them. OCSE staffs may also lack the time or resources to devote to custody cases.

Even more significant, you are not the OCSE lawyer's main client; the OCSE is. As long as the case involves just child support, your goals and the OCSE goals are identical: to collect support. Once custody enters the picture, however, you don't know if the OCSE has any goals about custody cases or what those goals might be.

In some OCSE offices, for example, change-of-custody requests by nonsupporting absent parents are generally viewed as an attempt to avoid paying support and are fought vigorously. Other offices, however, have an unspoken policy that the best resolution is the one that improves the children's financial status, or perhaps (viewed more cynically) the one that makes the case go away. If a wealthy nonsupporter wins custody and doesn't ask for child support, the case will be resolved and off the OCSE caseload, without financial loss to the children or the state. In other words, the OCSE lawyer may recognize the personal loss and disruption that a change of custody would cause but could also have conflicting goals. As a result, your case could suffer.

Clearly, your family stability is too important to risk to chance. Anytime a custody conflict arises, even if you already have an OCSE lawyer working on your case, you should consult an experienced independent lawyer.

It's helpful to know, incidentally, that a counterclaim for custody is unlikely to occur in a case pursued through URESA or through the criminal justice system. In URESA cases, you are protected by court decisions all across the country saying that URESA legislation was not intended to provide a new way to litigate custody and visitation questions but only as a way to collect support out of state. Similarly, in criminal nonsupport cases, complaints about custody would not be a proper defense and would therefore generally not be allowed into the case.

Of course, the noncustodial parent could still bring a separate action for change of custody in the appropriate family court. As a practical matter, however, many noncustodial parents who would use change of custody as a defense, counterclaim or bargaining tool in a support collection case won't be motivated actually to pursue a separate custody case. For this reason, it's helpful to bring your support claim in a court that won't reopen the custody question. Again, an independent lawyer can advise you in case of doubt.

FINANCIAL MATTERS

If the noncustodial parent has more than a moderate income (perhaps $20,000 a year or more), you may wish to consider using a private lawyer even in a nondivorce case. Particularly if you are seeking a child support order for the first time, an aggressive independent lawyer can help you avoid an unrealistically low support amount.

This is true for several reasons. First, both OCSE and URESA lawyers are used to dealing primarily with lower-income cases. This may change as the programs expand, but for now it tends to be true. Spending day after day working with lower income cases, these lawyers may tend to think in lower dollar amounts. As a result, they might in your case seek a child support amount appropriate for a much lower income noncustodial parent.

Even more serious, many states have entirely different systems for hearing OCSE or URESA cases than for hearing cases brought by independent lawyers. This means that not only the agency lawyers but also the judges or administrative law judges hearing the cases may be used to seeing lower-income cases and thinking in lower dollar amounts.

Additionally, a common problem in higher-income cases is the hiding of income or assets by a noncustodial parent who wishes to avoid his support obligations (see Chapter 11). There is a great deal that an independent lawyer can do about this problem, but much less that an agency lawyer can do. With heavy caseloads and limited staffs, OCSE or URESA lawyers simply may not have the time to spend on proving the true income level in just one case. They may also lack the experience, dealing as they do mostly with lower-income cases.

Also, the streamlined or "expedited" procedures now required by law for all state OCSE offices may be great for speeding up the average case but are problematic for the high-income case. While rules will vary from state to state, it's possible that many states will speed up cases by sacrificing some of the pretrial methods for discovering information about the other party. Similarly, many courts hearing URESA cases don't provide the same opportunities for pretrial discovery that a more traditional court would.

Unfortunately, those discovery tools are just what you need to prove how much support an upper- or upper-middle-income parent can fairly pay. If you seek help only from OCSE or URESA, you might lose your chance. By using an independent lawyer and the traditional legal system, however, you can have that opportunity.

VIOLENCE

If the noncustodial parent has ever been violent or abusive toward you or the children, there is even more than your financial security at stake as you seek child support. You need to know that you and the children will have your physical safety protected, too (see Chapter 14).

If you plan to collect support through the OCSE, you really

can't depend on its efforts to keep you safe from violence. As in custody cases, OCSE staff may try to help, but it's not the job they're trained to do. You may still want to have them pursue your child support case but seek independent legal help in taking steps to stay safe. If you do this, however, be sure to keep them informed of everything you do, because it will affect their handling of the child support case.

If you're getting a divorce, you should look for a lawyer who is experienced in divorce and custody cases, with as much experience as possible in violence and abuse cases. Your best bet for finding such a person is to contact a local hot line for battered women and their children. The staff there will probably know which local attorneys have shown the commitment and ability to handle cases like yours.

You could also check with a local Legal Services Corporation office, since some have excellent programs to assist battered women and children. If you call a Legal Services office and are told they have a long waiting period or don't usually handle divorce or support cases, be sure to tell them yours involves a violent noncustodial parent. Although all Legal Services offices have had to cut back their services in response to severe funding reductions, many will give priority to cases with a history of violence or abuse.

If you are living in a different state than the abusive parent and using URESA to collect support, you may not need private legal help. The mere physical distance may be enough to remove you and the children from danger. It's a good idea, however, to request that your address be kept secret during the URESA proceeding. In any event, you should be sure to let your URESA worker know there is a history of violence by the noncustodial parent.

If you are living in the same state but using the criminal justice system to collect support, you still may not need to have independent legal help. In fact, the criminal justice system is very experienced in dealing with violent individuals and may be much more effective at keeping you safe than a private lawyer would be. (That might be one good reason for you to choose the criminal nonsupport route; see Chapter 4.) Be sure to discuss your concerns and all past incidents of violence with the prosecutor handling your case, so that measures for your protection can be taken.

OTHER CASES

If your child support collection case involves none of these special problems, you may still be frustrated enough with agency red tape to consider trying a private lawyer. If so, your choice of whether to seek private legal help or use an agency remedy will simply be a matter of comparison shopping.

There's no reason to assume that an independent lawyer will always do a better job in a basic collection case than an agency lawyer will. Many OCSE offices, for example, have an excellent reputation for efficiency. It's also true that many private lawyers lack experience in support cases or may be too expensive for your budget.

There are, however, private lawyers who offer high-quality support-enforcement services at a reasonable cost. In recent years, their numbers slowly have grown—in part because improved collection laws have made support cases less time consuming, and in part in response to growing public demand. A few attorneys have even established successful high volume practices specializing in overdue support enforcement (with fees charged only as a percentage of the support that is actually collected).

FINDING A LAWYER WHO'S RIGHT FOR YOU

Finding a good lawyer is a great deal like finding a good restaurant. Your best bet is to begin by asking for suggestions among people whose judgment you trust and whose circumstances are similar to your own. Once again, a parents' group can be a good starting place.

You can also gather names of lawyers who handle child support enforcement by contacting your state or local bar association. Ask if they list lawyers by specialty areas and how much experience a lawyer must have in order to be listed. You can also ask if particular lawyers (both those they've named and any who were suggested by friends) have any disciplinary actions against them.

Yet a third source is useful if you are interested in a high-volume, low-cost law office. Some modern practices, often called legal clinics, may handle simple support cases quite efficiently but probably won't take more complicated cases, such as custody disputes. If you don't learn of any in your area through friends or the bar association, you can double-check by writing to the National Resource Center for Consumers of Legal Services, 3254 Jones Court N.W., Washington, D.C. 20007.

Once you've gathered a few names, you can begin calling the offices. Over the phone, you can ask about costs, experience and type of practice. This will help you decide whom you want to meet in person. Since many lawyers do not charge (or charge only a modest fee) for a first visit, you can keep looking if you don't feel comfortable with the first lawyer you meet.

Your first appointment will be a two-way interview. You'll be evaluating the lawyer, and he or she will be evaluating your case. Bring all your case information and expect to answer questions—but don't be shy about asking your own questions, too.

If you feel uncomfortable or intimidated, trust your own instincts. That's probably a sign that this isn't the lawyer for you. You deserve courtesy, clear explanations and an atmosphere of mutual trust and respect. If you don't get them, try elsewhere until you do.

If your case has special features, you'll want to ask about the attorney's experience with those specific problems. A case involving possible hidden income or assets of the noncustodial parent, for example, would require a lawyer with substantial experience in evaluating business and financial records.

For simple child support collection cases, some private lawyers will charge only if the case is successful, by taking a percentage of the support collected. This is called a *contingent fee* arrangement. It's a good way for you to get legal services you might not otherwise be able to afford and for the lawyer to bring in new business. A contingent fee arrangement can be a good indication that a lawyer has confidence in your case and will do the best job possible.

For a more complicated divorce or custody case, however, you may have to make other payment arrangements. Sometimes judges will require a higher income noncustodial parent to pay the custodial parent's lawyer fees, or a fee payment arrangement will be made part of a settlement agreement. If that doesn't appear likely, you may have to agree to pay a set fee, perhaps on a time payment plan. In any case, be sure you have a clear written agreement about fees in advance. It's also a good idea to comparison shop, because lawyer's fees do vary widely.

If you have a low income, you may qualify for free legal assistance from your local Legal Services Corporation office. In many areas, these programs offer excellent services. Unfortunately, due to recent federal funding cuts, most programs have been severely curtailed. Generally they can handle only the most serious cases, such as ones involving family violence or threats to an established custody arrangement.

Clearly there's no one right answer for every case. Before you make any decision, you'll want to ask, both at any agency offering services you need and of any lawyer you're considering as an alternative, what the costs are, what solid results can be expected and what the usual success rates are. It's also a good idea to ask other custodial parents what their experiences have been with either route, perhaps by attending a parents' group. You may get useful information and ideas, along with a dose of friendly encouragement as you make your decision.

6

Mediation: Does It Help or Hurt?

You may have heard of mediation, a very old method of resolving disputes that has recently gained popularity as a "new" way to settle divorce and support cases. Although family law mediation does have some good points, it also can present some very real dangers. Before you agree to mediation, you should be sure you understand exactly what it is and how it can affect your case.

In theory, mediation involves two or more people with a legal or personal dispute sitting down with a neutral third party to help them resolve the problem by compromise. In a divorce case, a mediator would work with the divorcing spouses to try to settle matters of property division, child custody and visitation, as well as alimony and child support. In a case involving child support only (for example, if the parents were never married and the father did not want custody), the parties and the mediator would focus simply on the amount and method of child support payment.

Some people turn to mediation because they think it's the only alternative to a knock-down, drag-out court fight. In fact, as we've seen, most family law disputes never go to court but are settled instead by lawyer-negotiated agreements. The few cases that actually do go to court are generally those in which one or both of the parties are absolutely refusing to compromise. So while neither lawyers nor mediators are *always* successful in persuading the parties to compromise and avoid a court fight, both are in fact able to do so in most cases.

In other words, the basic choice you are making is not between mediation and fighting it out in court. Your choice is whether to seek a negotiated settlement (assisted by your lawyer) or a mediated settlement (assisted by a mediator).

HOW MEDIATION AND NEGOTIATION DIFFER

One important difference between a traditional lawyer and a mediator is that the lawyer is paid to be your advocate, while a mediator is paid to be impartial. Thus in a traditional negotiation situation, your lawyer would try to guard your rights and get the best possible deal for you while the noncustodial parent's lawyer did the same for him.

The mediator's official function is simply to help the parties reach an agreement that both will accept and follow. While most mediators try to forge an agreement that will be fair to both parents, that's not really their job. Mediators, unlike traditional lawyers, have no duty to advise either parent on how best to protect his or her rights and interests in a case.

Many people who favor mediation feel it appeals to the parties' better natures, encouraging them to resolve their differences in a cooperative rather than a competitive manner. In many cases, that's true—as long as there's honest good faith on both sides. In families in which both parents place a high priority on the welfare of the children, mediation can be a good setting for working out the details of how they'll be raised. Parents can openly discuss their ideas about such matters as visitation, the children's education and so on, helping both parents feel involved in the child-raising process.

In some cases, noncustodial parents may feel good enough about that sense of involvement that they'll actually agree to pay more child support than they might have otherwise. Because they helped shape the agreement themselves, they may also respect and follow it more reliably.

Some families find that mediation can help them explore and resolve their feelings about a new family situation as they actively work to restructure it. Divorce, separation and the birth of a child are major life changes, and when mediation works well, it can provide a reassuring sense of control over one's life. In general, the more the parties feel resolved about the changes that have occurred, the more likely they are to respond positively to the new situation. That can make everyone's life easier, including yours and the children's.

It should be understood, however, that these happy results are likely *only* in cases in which both parents are truly concerned, involved and ready to place the children's needs above their own. Unfortunately, that's often not the case. All too often, as anger, defensiveness or even simple selfishness come into play, mediation can be used to gain an unfair bargaining advantage.

WHY MEDIATION CAN BE DANGEROUS

The mediator is not your advocate and has no obligation to advise you of your legal rights or of the consequences of a settlement agreement. That means that you could bargain away valuable rights without ever realizing you were doing so.

A common example of this problem involves child custody arrangements. Many mediators openly favor joint custody and, in fact, most mediated agreements do feature joint custody arrangements.

While joint custody may be an appropriate choice in many cases, it is certainly a decision with serious legal and practical consequences (see Chapter 13). It would be the legal duty of any attorney representing you in a divorce case to explain how agreeing to joint custody could create possible problems in terms of decreased child support, less control over decisions regarding your child or a potential custody conflict should you later need to move to a new state. A mediator would have no duty to explain these things and might even be unaware of them or feel that discussing them would interfere with the goal of reaching a compromise.

There's also an important practical problem, in that a mediator must, to gain the trust of both sides, avoid any appearance of partiality. This is fine if both parties are equally reasonable in their suggestions and requests but can create problems if there's an imbalance or a lack of good faith.

For example, suppose you were to start out making a fair and reasonable proposal, while the noncustodial parent made an unreasonable one. Had you privately told an attorney your goals, she or he might have said, "Well, that sounds fair. I'll ask for a little bit more and let them bargain me down." Had the absent parent done the same, his attorney might well have replied, "I'm sorry, but there's no way I can get you anywhere near that." Each lawyer would then have entered the bargaining arena with a proposal weighted slightly toward his or her client, but ready to compromise to reach a reasonable agreement.

Yet if, instead, you enter mediation with that fair proposal, while the absent parent makes his unfair one, the mediator will have a hard time getting much cooperation by saying, "Well, Mr. Jones, now that I've heard both sides, I really think you ought to agree to everything Ms. Jones suggests." More likely another kind of "compromise" will result—one somewhere in between your fair proposal and the absent parent's unfair one.

As you can see, there's a very basic problem here. You are urged, in mediation, to be fair, cooperative, even generous in resolving disputes. Yet as this example shows, if one person tries to be fair and the other doesn't, mediation may actually reward the unfair one.

POWER IMBALANCES

Any form of bargaining, to work well, requires roughly equal power between the two sides. That's why, for example, an individual laborer would not sit down to bargain over wage contracts with a large industrial employer. Instead, the employees band together in a union, hoping to equalize the power balance and get a fairer deal.

In domestic law mediation, there is an assumption of equal bargaining power that is often unrealistic. Any number of factors can create inequality between the parties and, overwhelmingly, they are factors that tend to favor men over women.

Men frequently have greater income and career mobility and more extensive knowledge of family financial holdings, and they may view any earnings or assets as "their" money (even if the family agreement was that the father would support the family financially while the mother raised the children). If a man was raised to believe he should be in control of his life, he may feel threatened by the loss of control over a failed relationship or the birth of an unexpected child. To reestablish that sense of control, or to act out anger, some men will try to dominate the bargaining process with power tactics and the withholding of support.

A woman, on the other hand, is still more likely to be the primary caretaker of the child or children and may place a high value on not angering their father. If the relationship has been stormy or difficult, she may be intimidated by the man's anger or his controlling tactics, or she may hope to restore peace in the family by not making too many demands. If she's been raised to believe that a woman should marry and keep the relationship strong, she may blame herself for its ending, feel guilty and not assert her own rights.

Particularly if you've been the children's primary caretaker and have limited financial resources, mediation could place you in a constant defensive position. In fact, you'll be supporting the children within your household and are asking only that the father contribute his fair share. If you are seeking alimony, it's in exchange for the work you've done and will continue to do raising your mutual children. Yet because you're asking for a sum of money—and because the work of child raising is so often undervalued in our society—you may be unfairly characterized as asking for some sort of gift or charity. It may be much harder for you to argue your cause in mediation than it would be for your lawyer to argue it in negotiation.

Before you agree to mediation, you should think carefully about whether any of the following questions apply to you:

- Are you the children's primary caretaker, and will you continue to be?
- Do you earn less or have more limited career opportunities than the children's father?
- Is the children's father more informed about financial or legal matters than you are, or more experienced at bargaining?
- Do you ever (or often) find yourself giving in to demands you know are unfair simply because it's too difficult or too unpleasant to persist?
- Do you ever feel afraid of or intimidated by the children's father?
- Do you find that conversations tend to be dominated by him, in that he seems to talk more and listen less?

Each one of these questions signals a possible problem area in terms of bargaining power. For every yes answer, you'll want to think carefully about whether mediation is right for you.

There are some circumstances in which you should *never* agree to mediation. If the noncustodial parent has ever been violent toward you or the children or been sexually abusive toward a child, mediation is not a good choice. You need the full protection of the law to keep yourself and your family safe and a good lawyer to put some distance between you and the noncustodial parent during negotiations.

You should also avoid mediation if you suspect that the noncustodial parent may have income, benefits or other assets that he's trying to hide and avoid sharing. As you'll learn in Chapter 11, there are many ways to solve this common problem and discover the hidden assets. Very few of these, however, are available in the mediation setting.

IF YOU DECIDE TO MEDIATE

Obviously mediation is right for some families and very wrong for others. If you favor its cooperative approach to problem solving and have a basic sense of trust in the fairness and honesty of the absent parent, you may wish to try it. If so, you'll want to follow some simple steps to use it as safely and wisely as possible.

The first and really unavoidable step will still be to start with a good lawyer to advise you about your rights in the case. You'll learn what kind of resolution you could expect if your case was handled through the legal system and what might be the consequences of any agreement you make, so you can bargain sensibly with these things in mind. If there are potential problems that make your case ill suited to mediation, a lawyer can help alert you to them. Also, since you'll still have to file court papers and have a judge approve any agreement you make, a lawyer can help you with that.

Above all, you should have any agreement checked by your lawyer (*not* just a lawyer acting as or with the mediator) before you sign or agree to anything. This is important, to be sure both that the agreement is fair and that it meets legal requirements of clarity and form. Most mediators are not lawyers, and even small mistakes can create problems later.

Fortunately this kind of low-level involvement by an independent lawyer is generally not too expensive. You can compare rates in advance simply by calling a prospective lawyer's office, explaining that you hope to reach a settlement through mediation and asking for a cost estimate for handling the case.

If, after discussing your case with a lawyer, you still feel mediation is right for you, your next step will be choosing a mediator. Possibly your lawyer will know of some reputable mediators, or a friend you trust may be able to recommend one. Mediation services are frequently listed in the telephone Yellow Pages under Mediation, Divorce, or Counseling, but a personal recommendation is always preferable.

The first questions you'll need to ask, before even scheduling a first appointment, are about background and training. This is essential for a very important reason. Because domestic law mediation is a fairly new field, most states have no legal requirements for mediators or procedures for licensing. This means it's up to you to be certain you are comfortable with the mediator's credentials. If you have any doubts or hesitations, you'd be wise to trust them and either seek a better-qualified mediator or stick to attorney-assisted negotiation.

Many mediators are trained and licensed as psychologists, clinical social workers or lawyers. Since each of these professions has licensing and disciplinary boards, you should check with the appropriate state board to be sure that the mediator you're considering is a member in good standing and has no outstanding disciplinary complaints on file. If your state has a separate licensing board for mediators (as of the end of 1984, none did), check with that board, too.

Another essential matter you'll want to ask about in advance is cost. While you probably won't be quoted a package price (since the total hours of mediation needed will depend in part on how quickly you and the noncustodial parent reach agreement), the mediator should be able to quote you hourly rates. Most mediators can also give you ballpark figures of how long average cases of your type usually take to resolve. While these figures will give you only an estimate or cost range, they are helpful in comparing costs with other mediators.

If you also want to compare costs between mediation and the traditional legal route, you can get similar cost estimates from lawyers' offices. When you are making your comparisons, remember to add in to the costs of the mediation route the expense of a lawyer to advise you of your rights and handle the court part of the process.

You may find that mediation is still less expensive. This is because negotiation is usually the most time consuming part of domestic law, and it tends to go faster in mediation. Also, in a lawyer-assisted negotiation, two lawyers are being paid for every hour they negotiate together, while in mediation, only one mediator is being paid during the session.

Questions about training and cost can be handled over the phone with the mediator's office, before ever meeting the mediator. Then, when you go for a first meeting with the mediator, you'll be able to focus more on questions about the mediator's attitudes and methods.

One good subject to ask about is the mediator's attitudes about families. Some mediators (male or female) accept social stereotypes that the household money is the man's money and may therefore not work to equalize the standard of living of all parties. Others may be so idealistic that they assume a level of cooperation and shared work that doesn't yet exist in most cases. They may, for example, assume that the children's father will share equally in child raising and that you will have ample career opportunities. If this isn't your family situation, that assumption can hurt you.

You might also want to ask whether the mediator thinks there can be power imbalances in a family and how they can affect mediation. The answer may be very interesting and will tell you a lot about what to expect. Be wary of any mediator who seems irritated by your questions or who insists that the problems don't exist.

Once you've chosen a mediator and are about to begin mediation, take some time to consider your mediation goals. Write down what you hope to accomplish, and discuss your ideas with your lawyer. Think about which issues are negotiable and which you see as nonnegotiable. The more clear you are in your own mind about what you and your children need, the more likely you are to meet those goals.

During the course of the mediation, try to be as businesslike as possible. Avoid unnecessary arguments, but don't hesitate to say so if you feel the noncustodial parent is being unfair or if you doubt he'll live up to some aspect of the agreement. Be honest about your feelings, but try to avoid letting emotional responses dominate the sessions. Instead, focus on your mediation goals, stating your needs and opinions as calmly and confidently as you can.

Because mediation involves bargaining, it's a good idea to ask for a bit more than you really want and then negotiate downward. Possibly your lawyer can help you set strategies.

You should be aware that the mediation process does not yet have many of the legal protections that have developed over the years to protect people during lawyer-assisted negotiation. For example, if you were to reveal private information during a lawyer-assisted negotiation session, it could not later be used against you in court. Yet the information could be used against you if your slip was during a mediation session. That may not be a reason in itself to avoid mediation, but it does mean you should avoid discussing such things as a new sexual relationship in your life during predivorce mediation sessions.

Additionally, the current lack of professional standards and disciplinary boards specifically for mediators can affect not only your choice of a mediator but also the handling of your case. It means that you have less leverage for protesting actions or policies that you feel are unprofessional or unfair, and that the mediator has less peer guidance for conducting cases. While this will probably change with time as the profession develops, for now, it is your responsibility to be sure you are satisfied of the fairness of mediation at every point. If you're not, you should discuss your concerns with your lawyer and, if necessary, withdraw from the mediation.

Clearly, your role in mediation is a delicate one. You're expected to interact in a basically open and honest way that will invite trust and cooperation, but you must avoid giving out information that could hurt you later if mediation fails. While making a good faith effort to be cooperative, you must nonetheless guard your financial status, for your children's sake as well as your own. You need to trust the other parent enough to be flexible, but you must not trust blindly or when the trust hasn't been earned.

If you find that tightrope dance too challenging or not suited to your family or personal needs, you're not alone. Yet for some families, the pluses outweigh the dangers. Neither the traditional legal route nor mediation has all the answers, and the best choice is the one that's right for you. If you think that choice is mediation, by all means proceed—carefully.

II

GETTING A
CHILD SUPPORT ORDER

7

Finding a Missing Parent

It's easy to be discouraged about collecting support if you don't know where the noncustodial parent lives or works. Unfortunately some parents do try to avoid their responsibilities by leaving town or disappearing from sight.

This trick used to work, but you don't have to let it now. The chances are good that you can track down the noncustodial parent, even in another state. All it takes is some initiative, some patience and a knowledge of the available resources.

THE PARENT LOCATOR SERVICES

A very good service for finding noncustodial parents is provided by the Federal Parent Locator Service (Federal PLS) and, in every state, the State Parent Locator Service (State PLS). The locator services are available to you through your state Office of Child Support Enforcement, and you can use them even if you don't plan to use any other OCSE services. If your family is not receiving AFDC, you will probably have to pay a modest fee ($25 or less) for the use of the parent locator systems. Some states have sliding fee scales, so you might be able to have the fee waived in a hardship case.

The state and federal PLS systems work together, making an extensive computer search of all available public records. If the noncustodial parent's home or work address shows up on any of the records, you will be notified and given the address(es).

The Federal PLS makes use of the following:

- Internal Revenue Service income tax records
- Social Security Administration annual earning records

- Social Security Administration benefit records
- Veterans Administration benefit records
- Department of Defense current duty station records
- National Personnel Record Center federal employee records
- Selective Service System draft registration records

State PLSs commonly use:

- state driver's license records
- state motor vehicle registrations
- state voter registration lists
- state employee personnel lists
- state Workers Compensation recipient records
- public assistance recipient records
- state prison records

In other words, if the noncustodial parent works, drives a car, pays taxes, receives any kind of government compensation or benefits or has engaged in any one of a number of activities from registering for the draft to going to jail, there's an excellent chance of finding him. In fact, in fiscal year 1983, the Federal PLS was able to provide a home address for the noncustodial parent in 70 percent of the cases sent to them and both a home address and an employer address in 50 percent of the total cases. Add to that the number of cases in which the noncustodial parent may show up on state PLS files (figures vary by state), and the picture is fairly encouraging.

To request a PLS search, simply call your local OCSE (listed under Resources). The people there will tell you when to come in for an appointment and exactly what to bring. Ordinarily, to show your right to have a search made, you'll be asked to bring your own driver's license or other valid identification, the child's birth certificate or other identifying documents and any documents showing your relationship to the child. To make the actual search, they'll also need the noncustodial parent's full name, any identifying information you may have about him and, if possible, his social security number.

The social security number is important, since most federal and many state records are accessed by use of that number. If you don't know it but have other identifying information (such as what kind of work the noncustodial parent does, what cities he might be living in or who his former employers were), the PLS service might be able to get it from the Social Security Administration.

Keep in mind that if the PLS doesn't come back with address information on the first try, you can always try again later. Record files are increasing all the time, as people get new jobs or new benefits or take on new obligations. Check with the worker handling your PLS case about procedures for repeating the search in a few months.

CONDUCTING YOUR OWN SEARCH

In the meantime, there's a great deal of helpful and perfectly legal sleuthing you can do on your own. As every good detective knows, you'll get results fastest if you explore every possibility, so your best bet is to file with the PLS and do your own homework, too. You may be able to find a work or home address for the noncustodial parent yourself or, if you don't already have it, find that social security number to speed the PLS search.

Perhaps you are in touch with some of the noncustodial parent's relatives or friends, who may know where he's gone or at least how to reach him in case of emergency. You may be able to enlist their aid. Some may be willing to help out of friendship to you or concern for the children. Others may be more guarded, wanting to "protect" the noncustodial parent, but may still give out bits of information they believe are unimportant. Some, such as former co-workers or casual acquaintances, may be willing to tell all they know (and may know more than you'd expect).

Obviously you'll have to play it by ear and feel out the best approach to each. You don't have to explain everything to everyone. You can quite truthfully say, for example, that you need to reach the noncustodial parent because there's a problem with the children. (There is: lack of support.) Or you could explain, in asking for the noncustodial parent's social security number, that you need it for a form for the children. (You do: the PLS search form.) Of course, be consistent if you're talking to people who will talk to each other.

Try to be as polite and chatty as possible with anyone you ask, even if relations have been strained in the past. You're more likely to get the cooperation you need and might incidentally pick up other bits of information that will be useful in your search. Whatever clues you hear, however casual or obscure, be sure to write them down.

Another likely source is former employers. Even an employer from several years back may have old personnel records that include employee social security numbers. A more recent employer may have been contacted for job references or may even have a current address for sending a last paycheck or year-end tax forms. Since many employers are reluctant to give out information over the phone, you'll probably want to make a personal visit.

Other, less commonly used sources may give out address information quite freely. With each of the following agencies or organizations, you would call and say politely and confidently, "Hello, I'd like to know if ——— is listed as a (member, customer, etc.). Thank you . . . And what do you show as his address and phone number, please?" If you are asked the reason for the request, you can simply explain that it is a personal matter regarding his children.

If you know what city the noncustodial parent is in, you may be able to locate him through utility companies. Customer service offices of local gas, electric and phone companies will all generally tell you if they have an account in a customer's name and at what address. You should also, of course, check the current phone book for that city. (Out-of-state phone books are available at most phone company offices and many libraries.)

Labor unions or professional associations (such as lawyer, architect, doctor, accountant or teacher licensing boards) are another generally available source of home and work address information. Similarly, if the noncustodial parent is a graduate of a college or trade school, the alumni association or placement office might have his current address and be willing to give it out to an "old school friend."

Even hobbies can be the key to finding address information. Bowling leagues, athletic clubs, civic organizations—whatever the noncustodial parent has done in the past and might do in a new city—are all worth contacting.

If the noncustodial parent disappeared within the past few months, you have still more possible sources of information. The post office may have a forwarding address, which you can obtain through a simple request form. If a car or van was rented for the move, local rental agencies may have records indicating the city in which it was returned. If traveler's checks were purchased, company records may show where they were later cashed.

Perhaps the noncustodial parent left with a checkbook or credit card from an account held jointly with you. If so, you're entitled to any account information. Bank records should show any change of address or interbank transfer, as well as where any checks were cashed or credit purchases made.

In many areas, the OCSE caseworkers will assist clients with this individualized search. If you want that help, ask when you apply for the state and federal PLS search.

Of course, you could also pay to have a search made privately. There are detective agencies that trace missing persons, but for the most part, they'll use the very same methods you would. Since your goal is to gain support and not to spend money unnecessarily, it generally makes more sense to do it yourself.

8

Establishing Paternity

If you were never married to the father of your child, you'll need to formalize the relationship between father and child before you can collect child support. It may also be necessary to have paternity acknowledged or established if your child was conceived after you and the father were divorced or born before you and the father were married. This is done either by the father signing a legal form that *acknowledges paternity,* or by a legal process called *establishing paternity.* Once paternity is acknowledged or established, your child will have the same rights to support, care and other benefits from the father as would a child born to married parents.

Many people, when they think of establishing paternity, imagine a long, tearful, embarrassing trial filled with angry testimony and lewd accusations. In fact, this grade-B movie image has almost nothing to do with reality. The vast majority of paternity determinations are settled by agreement, as fathers either willingly admit paternity or are persuaded to do so when blood tests and other evidence make paternity obvious. Even in the few cases that do go before a judge, paternity determinations tend to be reasonably private and straightforward, depending mostly upon objective facts such as blood tests and other evidence.

Most of the same people who can assist you in a child support action can also help you with a paternity determination. Probably the simplest and most confidential method would be to hire a good lawyer with experience in paternity determinations. Unfortunately that's also the most costly method. Blood tests may be quite expensive, as may lawyers' fees—and most lawyers require advance payment of both. While a judge in the case could eventually require the father, once he was determined, to reimburse you for these costs, many women find it impossible or too risky to advance the costs. So if you do decide to explore the idea of private legal help, be sure to discuss costs in advance (see Chapter 5).

Fortunately, the OCSE offers an effective, low-cost alternative. Many OCSE offices report a high success rate in paternity cases, with most cases settled by agreement with the father. As with other services rendered by the program, they are free to families receiving AFDC, while nonrecipients may be required to pay for some expenses (see Chapter 2).

There are also other options. If you have an out-of-state case you're planning to pursue through the URESA system (Chapter 3), you could check with your local URESA office to see if it would be better to have it process the paternity case instead of the OCSE. Similarly, if you'll be seeking a remedy through the criminal justice system (Chapter 4), prosecutors may be able to process the paternity case at no cost to you.

CASE PREPARATION

To begin your paternity case, a worker assigned to your case will ask you to come in for an interview and answer some questions about the father of the child and your relationship with him. Most of the questions will be quite ordinary: Who do you believe is the child's father? Where does he live? Where does he work? Has he ever visited the child or given gifts or money?

Other questions may be more personal. You will probably be asked, for example, how long your relationship with the child's father lasted, whether you had sex with him regularly and whether you were seeing any other men at the time you became pregnant. You may be asked when your last menstrual period was before you became pregnant and whether you had sex after that date with the man you've named as the father.

While it's natural to feel a bit uncomfortable discussing such personal matters with a near-stranger, you should understand that these questions are asked not to pry or criticize but simply to help you build a solid case.

Of course, not everyone is always sensitive and professional. For example, a small minority of OCSE offices will occasionally ask a mother seeking a paternity determination to submit to a polygraph (lie detector) test. Although they claim it helps weed out false claims, there's really no excuse for this practice. Clearly, no one is more interested in your case than you are, and common sense tells you that the workers need full and accurate information to proceed.

If you are at any time subjected to interview techniques you believe are inappropriate, by all means ask to see a supervisor to discuss the problem. If necessary, request that a different worker be assigned to your case or that an objectionable policy (such as the polygraph test request) be changed. Remember that the agency workers are there to serve you and just may not have realized that certain policies or approaches can be offensive.

After the initial interview, the lawyer or child support worker handling your case will contact your child's father by letter or phone. He'll be advised that he's been named as the *putative father*—the reported or alleged father—of your child. The worker will explain that the case could go to court, but it will probably be possible to avoid that by discussing it and reaching an agreement. The man will also be advised that he may hire a lawyer to assist and, if necessary, defend him. Since most men want to resolve the matter as quickly and quietly as possible, this conversation usually ends with the man agreeing to come to the worker's office (with or without a lawyer) to discuss the case.

Once they are in the office, different men respond differently. Some acknowledge paternity right away, out of a sense of responsibility. Some don't believe or aren't sure that they're the father and agree to blood tests in the hope of finding out the truth. Still others deny paternity out of anger or a desire to avoid their financial responsibilities but agree to blood tests only because they realize that the judge will undoubtedly order them anyway if a paternity action is filed. Very few persist in refusing either to acknowledge paternity or to submit voluntarily to blood tests (and, if they do, the tests can indeed be required by court order).

PATERNITY BLOOD TESTS

Modern blood tests (unlike earlier, limited ones) are quite sophisticated and very accurate. By analyzing blood samples from the mother, the child and the putative father, testers are able to show in each case either that the man is not the child's father or that there is an extremely high likelihood (up to 99 percent if more than one type of test is used) that he is the father.

Here's how blood testing works. All children inherit traits or characteristics from their parents, including traits that show up in the blood. Most of the traits are controlled by a pair of genes: one that comes from the father and one that comes from the mother.

In performing a blood test, the tester will look, one at a time, at certain traits that show up in the blood. If a trait shows up in the blood of the child but not the blood of the mother, that trait must come from the father.

If the man being tested doesn't have the trait, he can't possibly be the father. That's why even the simplest blood test can provide 100 percent proof that a man is *not* the father of a child. If a blood test is accurately performed and comes out negative, that's the end of the inquiry.

But suppose the tester looks at a given trait that the child has and the mother doesn't have, and finds that the man being tested does have the trait. Obviously this could just be a coincidence, so a single matching trait won't prove anything. However, if the pattern is repeated for a large number of traits—that is, if the man being tested has every trait that the child didn't get from the mother—it will indicate a high likelihood that that man is the father.

Early blood tests examined only a few traits and therefore were only of limited value in proving paternity. Today, however, there are three different types of paternity blood tests available, and each examines many traits to see if there's a father/child match. (See Notes, pp. 173–174, for a description of each test.[1])

To determine the exact probability that a man being tested is the father, testers use charts that show the statistical probability that a randomly chosen man would have all the matching traits that he does. By using two or more of the available tests, examiners can make an identification that is up to 99 percent certain. In legal terms, this is extremely effective proof that a man is the true father.

Keep in mind, too, that the statistical test results are based on biological similarity alone, not on any evidence of sexual activity. In other words, if you'd had sex with every man in town, that 99 percent probability of paternity would still be in effect.

In most cases, the man knows even before the testing starts that he had a sexual relationship with the mother and probably is the father. The blood testing merely acts as a confirmation of this, and he won't persist in denying paternity. Most likely, in fact, you won't have to have all three tests done, as most fathers will acknowledge paternity if the first or second test does not rule them out. Similarly, most judges would make a finding of paternity if there was evidence of a sexual relationship and at least two positive blood tests.

It's also reassuring to know that there is no real risk of making a false identification of paternity. If, for example, there were more than one man who could possibly be the father of your child, you could count on blood tests to rule one out and prove the paternity of the other. If this is a possibility in your case, be sure to discuss it with your lawyer or caseworker.

Due to out-of-date misunderstandings about the effectiveness of blood tests, a few states still don't allow them to be considered by a judge in deciding paternity. Check with the worker handling your case to make sure that isn't the situation in your state. If it is, ask how your case will be affected.

THE COURT PROCESS

As stated earlier, most paternity cases are settled by agreement and never go to court. On the off chance that yours is one of the few that does actually go before a judge to determine paternity, here's what you can expect.

Your lawyer (or a lawyer assigned to represent you) will present to the judge your evidence that the man is the father. You'll be asked to testify, in response to questions from your lawyer, why you believe this is the child's father. If you have any friends or family who knew about your relationship with the father or who later heard him say he was the father or saw him act as if he was the father, they can also testify.

The putative father will then be given an opportunity to testify, and he can have witnesses of his own testify, too. Your lawyer will be allowed to "cross-examine" (question) the father and his witnesses, and his lawyer will be allowed to cross-examine you and your witnesses. Additionally, the blood test results will be submitted as evidence and shown to the judge.

Based upon all the evidence, the judge will make a decision. If there are blood tests in your favor and no unusual problem with your case, you can be confident that the judge will find that the man is the father.

THE EFFECTS OF ESTABLISHING PATERNITY

Once paternity is established or acknowledged, your child and the child's father will have the same legal relationship that they would if you and the father had been married when the child was born. Your legal relationship to the father won't change, but the change in the father-child relationship can affect your family.

One important difference that many people don't think about is that once paternity is established, the father will have the same visitation rights as other fathers. He could even bring a custody claim, although in fact that rarely happens. Actually what visitation does occur seems to benefit most children (and there are probably more mothers who wish the fathers would visit more than wish they'd visit less). While you can certainly raise a happy, healthy child on your own, most children will also enjoy and profit from a positive relationship with their father.

You should be aware, however, that the father's rights as a parent once paternity is established could create problems later if he becomes abusive to the child. Your family would have the same protections it would if you'd formerly been married to the father, but no more (see Chapter 14). If you have reason to fear future abuse, you should not seek to have paternity established without first discussing your options with a private attorney who is experienced in family violence cases.

Another possible problem could arise if you later married a man who wanted to adopt your child. If the biological father objected, he could have more leverage to block the adoption if paternity had been established.

Clearly, it's important to consider in advance how the child and the family will be affected by the changes in the legal relationship between father and child. On a personal level, there may be advantages and disadvantages, and you'll want to weigh these carefully.

The financial and legal benefits to your child, once paternity is established, however, are quite clear and concrete. Your child will have the exact same rights to care and support as any other child. He or she will have the right to receive benefits in the father's name, such as social security or military dependent allotments; to inherit from the father equally with other children and, if desired, to use the father's name. Perhaps most important, your child will have the right to be supported by the father, beginning immediately and continuing through age eighteen.

9

The Legal Process

In order to collect child support, you'll need a legally recognized order that sets the amount and terms of payment. Child support orders are issued by judges, either to formalize an amount reached by agreement between the parties or to reflect the judge's decision after hearing evidence from both sides. The order may be the result of any one of several types of cases: an independent action for child support, a paternity case, a child abandonment case, a URESA support action or a divorce or legal separation.

If you and your spouse are getting a divorce or legal separation, there will probably be many things to decide and negotiate: child custody and visitation, property division, alimony and child support. In later chapters, we'll look at how the different parts of the divorce and separation process fit together and how you can best protect yourself and your children against financial loss. Obviously child support is just one part of that process, and it will be affected by each of the other decisions.

This chapter, which describes how the legal process works, focuses on the child support process. It will give you a basic idea of court procedure, whether your case is a divorce case or an independent action for child support.

You should be aware that this chapter describes the typical procedures available through traditional family courts. The streamlined or expedited procedures available through the OCSE may be shorter and simpler than the court process described in this chapter.

Here, step by step, is how the process works.

PETITION AND RESPONSE

Every legal action is started by preparing a legal document called a petition or a complaint. Depending on what kind of case you're pursuing, it might be, for example, a divorce petition, a paternity complaint or a criminal complaint charging child abandonment. Whatever type it is, it will state your name and address, the noncustodial parent's name and address, the relationship between the parent and the child and exactly what you are asking the court to do. Since you are seeking child support, the petition or complaint will specifically ask the judge to order the noncustodial parent to pay you that support.

Your lawyer (or the lawyer assigned to your case) will prepare the complaint in standard legal form, filling in the information that you provide. It will then be filed with the clerk of the court where the case will be pursued. The case will be given a number, generally known as a *docket number*, and from then on, that number will be used to make sure that all court papers regarding the case are filed together.

In order to give the court power, or what's called *personal jurisdiction*, over the noncustodial parent, it's necessary to have the petition delivered to the noncustodial parent personally. Generally the delivery is made (for a small fee) by a sheriff or other court official. If there are problems in making the delivery, you can usually arrange to have private "process servers," who charge a little more but are used to persisting, do it. Under the law, the noncustodial parent can't avoid the court's jurisdiction by refusing to take the papers or to answer the door. If he tries, the process server can just tack the court papers to the door, and the court will still have jurisdiction.

Personal delivery is only necessary to begin the case. All subsequent written communication about the case, from either you or the noncustodial parent, will again be filed with the clerk of the court, but copies will be sent to the other party by ordinary mail.

The noncustodial parent, after receiving the complaint, will have a brief period of time (commonly twenty days) in which to get a lawyer, if desired, and prepare a formal written answer. That time period can be, and often is, extended by request. If, however, the noncustodial parent fails either to request an extension or to file any answer within the time period allowed, you will get what is known as a *default judgment.* That means that you and your lawyer will be permitted to present your evidence as to the child's needs for support and the noncustodial parent's ability to pay, and the judge will decide on a support amount without hearing evidence from the noncustodial parent.

(Keep in mind that default judgments can work both ways. If you ever are served with any legal action—for example, an action for change of custody—it's essential that you contact a lawyer immediately so that the complaint won't go unanswered.)

CASE PREPARATION AND DISCOVERY

Assuming your complaint is answered, both you and the noncustodial parent will begin preparing your evidence and arguments for the child support issue. You'll prepare a budget of your own household needs and the needs of the child (Chapter 10), and you will gather information about the noncustodial parent's income and assets (Chapter 11). The noncustodial parent will probably also want to gather information about your income and assets.

The process for gathering information from the opposite party in a lawsuit is called *discovery.* It can be quite simple or very extensive, depending on the circumstances of the parties. For example, if the noncustodial parent's only income is from wages, verified pay stubs may be all that's needed to determine his income. If, however, he runs his own business, it may be necessary to examine and evaluate extensive business records to really know how much he earns.

There are several tools commonly used in discovery. They are available to both parties to the lawsuit and conducted under indirect court supervision. In other words, if you make an appropriate request for information and the noncustodial parent responds properly, the court won't get involved. But if the noncustodial parent fails to answer or answers dishonestly, he could be subject to penalties of fine or imprisonment for contempt of court.

These are the major discovery methods available:

- Request for production of documents. This requests accurate copies of specific documents relevant to the issues (such as financial statements, bank records, income tax returns and so on).
- Written interrogatories. These are written questions to the other party, which must be answered in writing and under oath.
- Depositions. These offer an opportunity for your lawyer to question the noncustodial parent (or the noncustodial parent's lawyer to question you) in person and under oath. All questions and answers are recorded by a certified court reporter for future reference.

Discovery can be time consuming and, if you're paying privately, expensive. It is important, though, because it gives you the information you and your lawyer will need to assert your case. As always, discuss costs versus benefits with your lawyer to decide how much and what kind of discovery will be a good investment. Also ask about requesting the court to have the noncustodial parent reimburse you for these and other legal fees.

NEGOTIATION

Once the discovery process is complete, the negotiation process begins. Your lawyer will meet with the noncustodial parent's lawyer—or you and the noncustodial parent will meet together with both lawyers—to negotiate a reasonable amount of child support. Most child support cases are settled by agreement and never go before a judge for a hearing. Ninety-eight percent of all divorce cases are settled by agreement,[1] for example, and the state of Oregon reports an equally high rate for settling paternity cases.[2]

In general, settling a case through negotiation is better than taking it to court. It saves on time and lawyers' fees and often helps avoid bitterness between the parties. Equally important, support awards reached by agreement are more likely to be paid reliably, without the need to return to court for enforcement.

All these advantages, however, should not keep you from insisting upon a fair agreement. If your lawyer is rushed due to too heavy a caseload, you may be urged to accept a less than satisfactory agreement just to save time. Don't do it. If you even suspect that might be what's happening, get a second opinion before making any decisions.

You also might face a situation in which the noncustodial parent knows you don't want to go to court and takes advantage of your reluctance by insisting upon unreasonable terms. Keep in mind that it's probably a bluff—he doesn't want to go to court and pay extra legal fees any more than you do. In the final analysis, getting a fair agreement you both can live with is more important than avoiding disagreement by accepting inadequate child support.

If you do reach an agreement, your lawyers will present the agreement to the judge and ask that it be made the judgment and order of the court. Unless the agreement is grossly and obviously unfair, the judge will probably agree. Once the agreement is made the order of the court, it will have the force of law. If the noncustodial parent later fails to live up to it, you will have the same remedies as if the judge had set the amount of support after a court hearing.

THE COURT PROCESS

If you can't reach an agreement and do have to go to court, here's what will happen. You, as the *plaintiff* or *petitioner* (the person who began the action) will have your case presented first. You will be asked to testify, under oath, about your income, the household needs and the child's needs. You'll be responding first to questions by your lawyer and may then be *cross-examined* (closely questioned) by the noncustodial parent's lawyer.

Your lawyer will review with you in advance the questions you're likely to be asked, in order to be clear about your answers. If you think it would help you to feel more confident, you can practice before the hearing by having a friend ask you the questions. Testifying is a little nerve-racking for most people, but it's really not so terrible. It's just a way of giving you a chance to explain your situation in an orderly (if somewhat controlled) manner. Try to be as direct and businesslike as possible, and you'll do fine.

After you testify, your lawyer will probably *call* (request) the noncustodial parent to testify. Again, most of the questions will be financial: how much does he earn, how much does he spend and on what. Your lawyer will try to show through the questions that the noncustodial parent is quite able to provide child support and is trying to evade his responsibilities.

Finally, your lawyer will *introduce into evidence* (show to the judge and make it part of the record of the case) any written documents gathered through discovery that show your financial status and that of the noncustodial parent.

After your case is presented, the noncustodial parent will be given an opportunity to present his case. He might testify again, this time responding to the more sympathetic questions of his own lawyer. He might also call other witnesses, such as family members or perhaps an accountant or a business bookkeeper, to testify about his financial status. Your lawyer will be allowed to cross-examine the noncustodial parent and each of his witnesses. If the noncustodial parent also has written documents to present, these, too, will be introduced into evidence.

At the conclusion of both cases, the two lawyers will each have a chance to argue briefly their client's cases to the judge. Your lawyer will explain how much support you are asking and why that's a fair amount, while the noncustodial parent's lawyer will probably argue for a lesser amount.

All this may sound very complicated and time consuming, but it needn't be. An efficiently presented case without special problems can often be completed in a few hours. A great deal depends on how well prepared the lawyers are and how willing everyone is to avoid acrimony and foot-dragging and concentrate on the issues.

Occasionally a case will have to be continued on a later date because the evidence is incomplete or the judge wants to review the evidence before issuing a decision. Most often, however, the judge will immediately issue an order setting the amount and terms of child support payments. This order may be a temporary order (for example, if there is an ongoing divorce and the property has not yet been distributed or final custody arrangements made) or a permanent order.

Even if the order is officially a final one, the judge will usually keep jurisdiction over the case. This means that the case can later be reopened at the request of either party. If there is a change in circumstances—for example, if the absent parent loses his job or gets a much higher paying one—either party may request a modification of the child support order. Also, if the order is not obeyed, you can come back and ask the judge to enforce it.

APPEAL

If you are dissatisfied with the court's final decision, you can appeal it to a higher court. The noncustodial parent also has this right. The higher court will not simply substitute its judgment for that of the lower court but will review the record from the lower court to see if there was any error in the proceedings. If there was, or if the higher court finds there was no evidence to support the lower court's order, the higher court will *reverse* the lower court's decision. This means it will no longer be in effect. Generally the next step will then be to schedule a new hearing. At the new hearing, the lower court will follow any directions of the higher court to be sure the original errors are not repeated.

10

Showing Your Family's Financial Needs

In most states, child support amounts are determined by balancing the needs of the children and the family unit against the ability of the noncustodial parent to pay support. To help determine your family needs, you'll be asked to prepare a projected monthly budget. It's important that you do this carefully and accurately.

Probably the most common mistake made in preparing a budget is underestimating costs. This can happen for a number of reasons. It's difficult to think in advance of everything your family will need each month, as so often there are unexpected expenses. Additionally, if you haven't been getting any support, you're probably used to getting by on bare-bones necessities and may hardly remember what a more reasonable budget is like. If you've been home caring for the children and will now be beginning a new job, you may not be aware of all the expenses you'll have for child care, transportation, work clothes, lunches, convenience foods and so on. Finally, you may fear being criticized for extravagance if you list expenses realistically.

In fact, it is expensive to raise a family, and your budget should reflect that accurately. According to U.S. government estimates, it will cost a family at a moderate income level ($20,-000 to $40,000 a year) a total of $159,430 (or an average $8857 a year) to raise a child born in 1980 to age eighteen. Those figures, which assume a two-parent household with one parent home raising the children, include only out-of-pocket expenses spent to meet the children's basic needs. They do not include day care or after school care costs; neither do they budget anything for a college education or other post–high school training.[1] Clearly, when you see objective government figures documenting the high cost of child raising, it doesn't make sense for you to be limited to a subsistence-level budget.

The lawyer or child support worker handling your case will probably have a budget form for you to fill out. It will list many common expenses, and you should use it as a starting point in listing yours. To help you make sure you include everything, there's also a budget checklist included in the appendix of this book.

You could start with the budget form your lawyer gives you, check to see if anything from the list here should be added and then do a third check by thinking carefully about your family's special needs. If you have an old checkbook or other financial records, these can help jog your memory. Finally, you might want to brainstorm with a friend or family member to be sure nothing is left out.

As you put together your budget, concentrate on reflecting your family's needs as completely as possible. Expenses you have now should be included, of course, but so should the things your family really needs but hasn't been able to afford without adequate support from the noncustodial parent.

Most budget forms are done on a monthly basis. You can convert any expenses you pay weekly by multiplying them by 4.33, and any expenses you pay every other week by multiplying by 2.17. (This is because there are 4.33 weeks to a month, not just 4.)

Expenses you pay once a year should also be divided by 12 and included. A few examples might be property and other taxes, summer camp or vacation, school clothes in the fall, warm coats for the winter and so on. It's difficult to think of all these things, but it's worth the extra effort.

Of particular importance are any unusual expenses or special needs your family might have. If you or one of your children requires care for a medical condition, for example, this means that you'll have expenses that most other families don't have.

The same is true of educational or social needs, whether for a learning-disabled child or one with unique talents that should be developed.

By clearly showing these extra costs, you make it more likely that the noncustodial parent will agree to a higher level of support. Or, if the case is eventually decided by a judge, the judge will have a clear picture of the special needs. Even if the court or agency handling your case uses standardized charts to determine child support levels, these special needs may be considered and may result in a higher support award.

Over the next several years, we will almost certainly see more and more use of standardized charts for determining child support amounts. In fact, one of the requirements of the federal Child Support Enforcement Amendments of 1984 is that states organize special commissions, with citizen participation, that make recommendations on standardized child support charts and other matters related to child support and custody.

In general, standardized charts are a good idea, because they can save time and promote fairness. They reduce the possibility of bias and prejudice in the court system, since the judge has less leeway in setting awards, and may also encourage out-of-court settlements by making the outcome more predictable.

Whether the charts themselves will be fair overall, however, is another question. Unfortunately, many states appear to be leaning toward what are called *cost-sharing* standards for determining support levels, a method that has been highly criticized by several experts as being unfair to women raising children.[2]

Different states have different exact formulas, but here is the basic idea of how the cost-sharing method works. The court starts with a standardized estimate of how much it costs to raise a child each month. If the noncustodial parent is earning half of the family income (that is, if the two parents have equal salaries), the noncustodial parent will pay as child support half of that assumed cost of raising the child. If he's earning two-thirds of the family income (if he's earning twice as much as the custodial parent), he'll pay two-thirds of that cost, and so on.

This method may sound fair on first impression, but it has some real problems. First, the amounts used as the assumed cost of raising a child tend to be extremely low, because it's difficult to document costs accurately and separate them from general household costs. In case of doubt, there's a real tendency to let the costs be paid where they occur—that is, to leave them to be paid by the custodial parent. As a result, a child support figure that will in theory meet one-half or two-thirds of the child's needs will often *in fact* meet only a small portion of actual needs. Note, for example, that despite the government reports showing the moderate cost budget for raising a child to be $8857 a year, the mean amount due to custodial mothers with child support orders in 1981 was $2460.[3]

Second, and more fundamental, the cost-sharing method places absolutely no value on the work of child raising. Instead of a family system in which one parent does the primary work of child raising while the other does the primary work of financial support, we now have a system in which one parent (the custodial mother) still does the major work of child raising but is now also asked to share equally in the financial cost. It's sort of like suggesting that a wife become "liberated" by taking out the garbage half the time—while continuing to do all the family cooking.

Critics of this method have proposed the much fairer *income-equalization* method.[4] This method, unlike the cost-sharing method, does not even attempt to separate the cost of child raising from the larger costs of the family unit. Instead, it uses standardized government standard-of-living charts, which show comparable income ranges for families of different sizes. Using this method, a judge would look at the total family income and determine how it should be divided to put each of the new family units at the same standard of living. Child support (or child support and alimony combined) would then be set at the level necessary to accomplish this goal.

It's helpful to know all this because, if your state has not yet developed firm child support formulas, your lawyer may be able to argue in favor of the income-equalization method. Even if your state does have charts based on the cost-sharing method, they will probably show only a recommended range for child support awards, not a single prescribed figure. Your lawyer may be able to argue that the amounts shown on the chart would be unfair in your case if they would leave you and the children with a standard of living much lower than their father's.

In other words, you'll be using a combination of advocacy and advance preparation to meet your goals. Your lawyer will argue for basic fairness and may directly or indirectly draw upon income-equalization principles to show what's fair. That, combined with your carefully prepared budget showing the actual costs of raising your children, will help you secure the support your children need.

11

Finding Hidden Income and Assets

It's impossible to negotiate a fair agreement if you don't know exactly how much the noncustodial parent earns, how much he has to spend and how much he owns. Some noncustodial parents, trying to avoid child support payments, will hide income and assets that should rightfully be shared. This is particularly a problem in divorce cases, where not only child support but also property division and possibly alimony are at stake.

At greatest risk, inevitably, is the traditional trusting wife. If that's your situation—if you've been raising the children and leaving family financial matters to their father—you may not know exactly how much he earns. He may be self-employed, taking in thousands of dollars under the table that are never reported on income-tax returns. He may be a salesman earning commissions and investing some of that commission money privately. His company may give him an expense account that pays for his car, many of his meals, even his entertainment. There are any number of ways he may look cash poor and unable to support the children, while he's in fact enjoying a quite comfortable standard of living.

Unfortunately many lawyers who regularly handle divorce and support cases simply aren't aware enough of the problem of hidden income and assets or diligent enough in fighting it. They may ask for the financial records but do nothing to make sure they're accurate. Or if they do get the records, they may not know how to analyze and use them properly.

What's more, some of the newer methods of handling divorce and support cases practically ignore the problem altogether. In Chapter 9, you learned about the discovery process under the traditional legal system, which provides the tools that make it possible to discover hidden assets. Yet the expedited procedures now required under the federal Child Support Enforcement Amendments may in many states mean sacrificing the discovery process in OCSE cases. Similarly, most mediators depend on honest voluntary disclosure of income and assets, without double-checking against available financial records. Clearly, if you think hidden assets may be a problem in your case, you'd want to think twice about using either of these forums.

What can you do to protect yourself? If you have any reason to suspect hidden income or assets, you'll need a lawyer who is experienced both in legal discovery methods and in financial analysis. Some lawyers work on hidden-asset cases in cooperation with other experts as needed: corporate accountants if business records need reviewing, real estate experts if income-producing property needs appraising and so on. This is a good practice and can make an enormous difference in the final settlement of property division and continuing support.

Of course, top-notch lawyers and other experts can be expensive, and that's always an important consideration. Yet you need to balance that expense against the fact that assets that remain undiscovered are assets you and your children will never share.

If, for example, you are married to a man who is working as a waiter and you believe he's likely to understate his tips, it probably wouldn't make sense to spend much on discovery about that. Instead, you could make your own estimate based upon what he's brought home in the past and what he appears to buy from the surplus. It would be your word against his, but if you kept reliable records for a few weeks, that would be a big help.

On the other hand, if your husband is a corporate executive earning $30,000 a year or more, with extensive benefits that supplement his income, that's an entirely different situation. Spending the money to establish exactly what he earns, what benefits he receives and where any surplus is hiding is an essential investment in your financial future. The cost difference between incomplete and complete discovery may be a few hundred or even a few thousand dollars; but in a serious hidden asset case, incomplete discovery could cost you far more in settlement dollars.

Keep in mind, too—and discuss with your lawyer—that lawyer and other expert fees need not come straight from your pocket. If the discovery is part of a divorce-settlement process, your lawyer could seek fees from your husband or from the marital estate. Even if it's only a child support action, you can still bargain for or ask the judge to award payment of attorney fees by the noncustodial parent.

TRACKING DOWN FINANCIAL RECORDS

You can also save money on discovery and maximize your chances of getting accurate documents if you plan ahead. It's very important that you be as aware as possible of family finances and business and other financial records.

There are several kinds of financial statements used to detect hidden income and assets. Here are some of the most common:

- past and present income-tax returns
- savings account records
- checking account records
- money market accounts
- stock records
- loan applications
- real estate records
- business capital-asset reports
- business profit-and-loss reports
- business daily books (collections and disbursements)
- personal and business expense accounts

Each of these documents is useful in its own way. Loan applications, for example, are valuable because they tend to list many or all available assets, since the applicant is trying to impress the lender with his solid net worth. Other documents are helpful because they tend to show yearly or monthly income.

If you are married and not yet separated, many essential documents may be available to you from files in the home or the family business. The simplest and most direct method of obtaining them is to make photocopies quietly and privately.

You may not feel comfortable with this, and of course it's your decision. But keep in mind that family financial papers are your papers, too. If your husband doesn't ask your permission to use the family files when you're not around, there's really no reason you have to ask his.

Unfortunately, important papers have a way of getting lost or even altered as the divorce process progresses. Divorce lawyers tell stories of about-to-be-ex-husbands with two sets of books: the real ones and the ones left around for the wife to find. While some men keep phony books for years before divorce is even discussed, most do not. Obviously, timing and discretion are key. The sooner you can make copies of available financial records, the less likely they are to have been altered.

There are, of course, other ways to gather the records needed to track down hidden income and assets. The legal discovery tools, particularly requests for production of documents, are very helpful for getting business and other records. Other discovery tools, such as written interrogatories or depositions, are a good way for an experienced lawyer to ask leading questions and find out all kinds of helpful information.

Some documents will be held by third parties. If you are a joint signer on a bank account, you can obtain account records directly from your bank. Similarly, you could request copies of old forms you jointly signed such as loan or credit card applications. Official copies of joint income-tax returns for the past six years may be obtained by request to the Internal Revenue Service. (Ask for Form 4506, "Request for Copy of a Tax Return.") Your lawyer could help you with these, of course, but you can save time and money by doing the footwork yourself.

The most successful searches for hidden income and assets

are generally those that use a combination of all the available methods: your own collecting of records, the legal discovery methods and requests to third parties. Even if there is some slight duplication of effort, it can have unexpected advantages.

Occasionally, for example, a conflict between copies of the same record will appear, providing a clue that there has been some tampering. That's a direct help in finding hidden assets, of course, but it's also important in another way. Record tampering is a serious matter, both because it indicates that the tamperer is trying to cheat the other party and because it is considered a fraud on the court. If you can show the judge that it is happening, that fact will almost certainly be considered in making any property division or support award.

HOW HIDDEN INCOME AND ASSETS ARE DETECTED

Hidden income—money or other benefits regularly received but not reported to the other spouse—can sometimes be detected directly by examining business or other financial records. Day-to-day business records, for example, might show a greater profit than was originally reported in income statements. They may also show unreported benefits, such as a company car, travel expenses, meals purchased at company expense and so on.

Some kinds of income, such as cash payments for unreported work, won't appear on any records anywhere. Yet if an analysis of spending and savings—using bank records and records of other assets such as stock or real estate purchased—shows that significantly more money is being spent than is reportedly being earned, that, too, is evidence of unreported income.

Suppose, for example, that your husband reports a net after-tax income of $20,000 in 1984. Yet deposits to his checking account that year total $18,000 and deposits to savings total $5000. Unless he can provide some other explanation, it would appear that he has at least $3000 in unreported income.

Hidden assets—investments or property owned but hidden

from the other spouse—may also be uncovered with a little detective work. Sometimes it's merely a matter of knowing the right questions to ask. For example, future pension rights are important assets that should be considered in any property division, but they are rarely reported in response to a simple request to list all assets. A more specific written request, however, to the spouse or to his employer, will generally bring pension rights to light.

Deliberately hidden assets may also be detected by analyzing available financial records (and tapping your own knowledge and memory). One common method is to trace assets that were previously known to exist but are no longer evident.

For example, suppose you recall that your husband sold jointly owned stock two years ago for about $20,000. Yet an analysis of bank records and other investments for that year shows an increase in net worth of only about $13,000. Simple arithmetic shows that some $7,000 has mysteriously disappeared. While there may be a perfectly innocent explanation, such as taxes paid or unusual expenses, there often is not. At that point, close questioning by your attorney might uncover an undisclosed investment or bank account dating from that time.

Another clue to finding hidden assets is unexplained income, however small in amount. For example, suppose your jointly filed 1984 tax return indicates interest income of $380. It would be simple enough to assume that was interest from your joint bank accounts, but an examination of known bank record shows that interest on those accounts totals only $200. That inconspicuous $180 difference could be due to an unreported $3000 bank account (paying out 6 percent interest yearly).

Although you need a lawyer and probably an accountant qualified in financial analysis, don't just turn the job over to the experts and leave yourself out of the process. You'll have a lot to contribute that they need to know: knowledge of your husband's life-style and habits, memory of past investments and so on. You should definitely plan to meet with your lawyer and any other experts to help evaluate all documents.

Finding hidden income and assets is a complex task at times, but it's an important one. By working closely with qualified, dedicated professionals, you *can* succeed. Remember that every hidden dollar is one that was earned with the support of the family and stolen away from it in the hiding. By bringing these family assets to light, you help to secure a fairer division.

If the divorce or child support process is completed and you later learn of assets that were hidden, it is possible to have the judgment or agreement set aside for fraud. Unfortunately, this can be difficult and expensive. It's a good idea, therefore, to work as hard as you can to discover all income and assets *before* beginning divorce and support negotiation.

12

The Truth About Alimony

There's a common myth in our society about women who receive alimony, and it's as colorful as it is inaccurate. Alimony recipients, according to the stereotype, are happily living the high life on their ex-husbands' hard-earned money. If they aren't dressing in mink and dancing until dawn, they are lazy and unliberated, preferring a life of potato chips and soap operas to an honest job. Either way, they dress their children in rags and buy expensive presents for their new boyfriends. And these happy alimony recipients, it is widely believed, constitute the majority of divorced women. They receive alimony just because they are women (in a case of blatant discrimination against men), without any showing of need or service to the family.

In fact, nothing could be further from the truth than this offensive stereotype. To the contrary, the vast majority of divorced women do *not* receive alimony, despite their years of service to the family and the fact that they usually continue to do the major work of child raising. Even those few who are awarded alimony tend to receive amounts so low that they are still left with a standard of living much lower than that of their ex-husbands.[1]

If you've been the major caretaker for your children and acted as homemaker for the family, you've performed valuable services that deserve to be compensated. It is no more "unliberated" for you to seek alimony than it is "unmanly" for a businessman to expect a pension.

87

WHY ALIMONY IS IMPORTANT

In many cases, alimony is essential to a fair division. Your husband's earning power has probably increased over the years, in large part due to the fact that he's been able to concentrate on his career instead of on other family responsibilities, while yours may have declined or not been developed *because* of your family responsibilities. That may be a division of labor that worked well for your family in good times. Yet it's important to see that your husband's increased earning power is an important family asset that should be shared.

In fact, alimony is simply a practical way of sharing what may in fact be the most substantial financial asset that you as a family have. Many if not most divorcing couples have little actual cash or property to divide but depend on the husband's earning power to pay bills and make purchases. One study shows, for example, that among the middle- and lower-income families who constitute half of the divorcing population, the median value of all their property at divorce time was typically equal to only three months of family income.[2] Clearly, to simply divide that "three months' worth" of property—but leave the husband with years of enhanced earning power because his career advanced while his wife raised the children—would not be a fair division.

You should also understand that alimony always has had the function of supporting not only the homemaker but the household unit as a whole. Until recently, it was often favored over child support, for a very simple reason: alimony is tax deductible for the person who pays it, while child support is not. Since the breakup of a traditional male breadwinner–female homemaker family would leave the man in a higher tax bracket, alimony was a good way for the man to save money by transferring income from his high tax bracket to the woman's lower one. (This is still true, and a detailed explanation follows in the tax section.)

In the past, therefore, divorce agreements were commonly structured with very low child support payments and comparatively high alimony payments. In fact, both sums helped make it possible for the children to be raised adequately, but the actual choice of alimony rather than child support was made for tax reasons. In effect, alimony served in part as a sort of tax-deductible child support, while actual child support was kept artificially low.

More recently, as alimony fell into disfavor, an alarming trend developed. More and more divorces were granted without any alimony at all, but child support levels were not raised from their artificially low levels. (To the contrary, between 1978 and 1981, child support levels in inflation-adjusted dollars actually decreased 16 percent.[3]) In effect, women are being asked to raise children on sums that were never intended to reflect the true cost of child raising.

This history of the problem, while it is discouraging, is important to understand. If you are seeking alimony, your lawyer should recognize the important social policy reasons behind it and be ready to advocate on your behalf. Equally important, he or she should have a clear sense of all the ways in which you and your husband have worked cooperatively over the years to succeed together. Less important than who has done which tasks or earned what sums is the fact that you've both done your share, according to the agreement between you. If divorce now leaves him with the greater earning power, it should not leave you behind in relative poverty.

Even if you are not seeking alimony, your lawyer should understand the historical connection between alimony and child support and be ready to assert and justify a claim for a reasonable level of child support. You should not be limited to the artificially low levels of child support that were used as standards in the past, when it was assumed they would be supplemented by alimony.

Discuss these issues with your lawyer at least briefly. Not all lawyers understand and are willing to advocate vigorously for alimony and realistic child support levels, so you need to be sure yours is.

At the same time, you should realize that even the most idealistic lawyer is limited by what is realistically possible within the system. Due to the growing prejudice against long-term alimony (not to mention the difficulties of enforcement), it might be wise to consider alternatives. Cold cash in the bank may be a safer bet than a promise to pay, particularly if you sense that your husband might be unreliable in meeting support payments. If you've been away from the work world for a while, you might seek short-term alimony so you can go back to school and update your credentials. If you have young children and sense that their father is more likely to support them reliably than to "give" you anything labeled alimony, seeking a realistic level of child support might be a wiser priority.

In other words, you and your lawyer should project a firm, unapologetic message that you've contributed your fair share to the family and deserve a fair share of the financial returns. Yet in structuring exactly how to do that, you'll need a certain amount of flexibility and even creativity. By working closely with a lawyer you trust and respect, you can increase your chances of reaching your financial goals.

Although child support and alimony often serve a similar function and may even come together in a single check, they have important practical differences. These differences can affect your family finances, so it's good to be aware of them.

LEGAL EFFECT

One main difference between alimony and child support is the period of time that each will ordinarily continue under the law. Unless otherwise specified in a court order or agreement, alimony generally continues until the recipient remarries or either party dies. Child support continues until the child being supported reaches majority (age eighteen in most states) or is *emancipated.* Generally, *emancipation* means the child is married, joins the military or leaves home and becomes self-supporting.

These limitations can generally be changed by agreement, and in many cases they should be. In Chapter 15, you'll learn about the ways you can customize your agreement to fit your family's needs, but for now, it's helpful to know when alimony and child support will each end if you don't make a special agreement.

TAXES

Another basic difference between alimony and child support is their tax consequences. Specifically, you should be aware that you'll have to pay income taxes on any alimony you receive. Your ex-husband, however, will be able to deduct the alimony payments and save on taxes.

Suppose, for example, that you and your divorcing spouse agreed he would pay you $3000 a year in alimony. If your income (including that alimony) puts you in a 20-percent tax bracket, you would be required to pay a total of $600 in taxes on that alimony income. Your *net gain* would be only $2400 ($3000 alimony − $600 tax = $2400 net gain).

Your ex-husband, on the other hand, would be able to deduct the alimony payments from his income for tax purposes. If he is in a 40-percent tax bracket, for example, he would save $1200 in taxes each year. This means that his *net cost* of paying that alimony would be only $1800 ($3000 alimony payment − $1200 tax savings = $1800 net cost).

Note that in this example, the net gain to you ($2400) would be greater than the net cost to your ex-husband ($1800). This is what we mean when we say that alimony promotes tax savings. It does not mean that *you* will save directly on taxes—in fact, you'll be paying the entire tax cost on that alimony income. It simply means that your ex-husband's tax savings may be greater than your tax cost. This can help you, however, by making a higher alimony payment more affordable for your ex-husband.

Child support is different in that it has no tax consequences. A $3000-a-year child support payment would mean $3000—in net gain to you and your children and in net cost to their father.

The different tax treatment of alimony and child support does not necessarily mean that one is always better than the other. It's just that you and your lawyer should be aware of exactly what you're getting in *after*-tax dollars and always bargain with this in mind.

If you do receive alimony, whether it's temporary or long-term, you will probably be required to file estimated income tax payments every three months with the Internal Revenue Service (IRS). This is because we have a "pay as you go" tax system, and you're not allowed to wait until the end of the year and pay your total tax bill. (At your job, your employer withholds and sends in your estimated taxes, but for alimony and self-employment, you must do it yourself.) To enforce this rule, the IRS imposes stiff cash penalties on those who fail to make their quarterly payments, so be sure to pay on time.

To determine if you'll need to file estimated taxes, write or call your local IRS office and ask them to mail you Form 505 on Estimated Taxes. If you have questions, contact the IRS or ask your lawyer or accountant.

Although you'll be taxed on your alimony income, you will be allowed to deduct any expenses incurred seeking or enforcing the collection of that alimony. For this reason, you should be sure that your lawyer itemizes any bill to you. Any portion of the bill related to negotiating or enforcing alimony will be deductible, as will court costs related to collecting alimony. Additionally, if your lawyer bills you for tax advice, that portion of the bill will also be tax deductible.

ENFORCEMENT

The final important difference between alimony and child support is that alimony can be even more difficult to collect. In 1981, only 47 percent of the women who were due child support received the full amount; but an even lower 43 percent of those who were entitled to alimony collected the full amount.[4] With the recent federal emphasis on child support enforcement, we can hope to see child support collections improve, but it's less certain that alimony will follow suit.

The popular prejudice and misunderstanding about alimony is probably the major reason for the difference. As long as alimony is not understood and appreciated for the important role it plays within the family, its enforcement will probably continue to be lax. We are finally seeing judges who will withhold wages to collect child support and even jail the most flagrant offenders, but alimony enforcement is rarely taken this seriously. No one wants to be seen as being unconcerned about children, but that concern seems not to extend to their caretakers.

Traditionally, enforcement methods have generally been equally available (at least in theory) for collecting child support and alimony. Yet even this may change. The improvements in child support enforcement methods required by the federal Child Support Enforcement Amendments of 1984 are not specifically required to apply to alimony collection as well. Quite possibly, given the common prejudices against alimony, some states will not extend the improved collection methods to alimony collection (unless, of course, there's a strong lobbying effort to see that they do).

Additionally, some agency enforcement services may be less available to you if you are awarded only alimony and no child support. At present, state Office of Child Support Enforcement programs are not required to offer their services for collecting alimony unless there is also child support needing collection.

Similarly, most states will not pursue an interstate URESA action to collect alimony unless there is also a child support case. Both of these policies could change, but for now, you need to be aware of them.

There are, obviously, advantages both to alimony and to child support. You may wish to seek a combination of the two, or a combination of both and a property division. As you think it over and discuss it with your lawyer, feel free to ask questions and express your opinions. You, after all, are the one who will live with any agreement you make.

13

Child Custody

As you make decisions about child custody, you'll certainly want to consider your own emotional needs and those of your children. Yet custody decisions have important legal, practical and financial consequences, too. These also affect your children's welfare, and you need to know about them to make the best possible decisions.

There are a number of books and articles available today that look at the emotional factors involved in custody decisions. This chapter, which focuses on the practical aspects of custody, won't attempt to repeat them. Instead, we'll look at how custody arrangements can affect your family's future security in terms of living arrangements, support levels and future efforts to collect needed child support.

Although it is possible to have a custody conflict when the two parents have never been married, most custody questions arise in divorce or postdivorce cases. For that reason, this chapter focuses on divorce situations. Because widespread trends in the legal system can affect your case, a general look at past and present trends is included.

The term *custody* actually has two meanings: *legal custody* and *physical custody*. The *legal custodian* of a child is the person with the right and responsibility to make decisions concerning the child's living arrangements, education, social activities, health care and so on. The *physical custodian* is the person who lives with and cares for the children on a day-to-day basis.

As a general rule, it's best if legal custody reflects the actual physical custody arrangements. If you've provided the majority of care to children in the past and expect to continue doing so, you should seek legal custody of them. It will allow you to make decisions ranging from where you and the children will live to what rules will be followed in your house—and to do so without fear of contradiction by the noncustodial parent. Your rights, of course, will be tempered by the noncustodial parent's rights to visitation, and the welfare of the children will be considered first in any dispute. Yet on a day-to-day basis, as you care for the children, having legal custody will allow you to make decisions and exercise the leadership and moral authority you need to parent effectively.

Child support is another important reason to seek legal custody if you'll actually be caring for the children. If their father becomes the legal custodian, you're more likely to have to pay child support than to receive it, even if you care for the children much of the time.[1] Even if the legal custody is joint, child support awards tend to be low or nonexistent, even when the *actual* care of the children follows traditional lines (with the mother providing primary care and the father exercising visitation). Then, if you turn to AFDC to ease your economic burden, you may find you have difficulty obtaining it because you don't have sole legal custody.[2] Apparently both judges and AFDC officials tend to assume that joint legal custody will mean equal child raising responsibilities, when in fact it means only equal decision-making rights.

Finally, legal custody arrangements that reflect the actual physical caretaking are important because they tend to produce stability and protect against later change-of-custody *(modification)* actions. For example, if you receive legal custody of the children at divorce or separation time and continue to provide them with primary care in your home, it will be relatively difficult for the other parent to have custody switched to him later. At a minimum, he'll have to show a change of circumstances making the change in the best interests of the children. Equally important, the judge will be more likely to recognize your role as primary caretaker and be reluctant to disrupt the children's lives with a total custody switch.

If, however, you provide most of the child care but agree at divorce time to call it joint custody, it will be much harder later on to show that a switch to sole custody by the children's father will really be such a disruption. The judge may assume that the father has already been providing a great deal of the care, and it may be difficult for you to overcome that assumption. Worse yet, if you do manage to show you've been providing most of the care, the judge may even suspect that the child-care split is uneven because you've been preventing the children from seeing their father regularly. Particularly if there *has* been a change of circumstance that makes the father look more stable or successful—for example, if the children's father has remarried and you haven't, or he has a house and you're living in a cramped apartment—the result could be a switch from joint custody to custody by the father.

In other words, who will be the primary caretaker of the children or whether caretaking responsibility will be divided between the two parents is a largely emotional decision, based upon your own family history, personalities and needs. But you need to be sure, for your own protection and that of your children, that the legal custody arrangements accurately reflect the actual, workable plans. In short, if you'll be raising the children, you should be their legal custodian.

HOW CUSTODY IS DECIDED

Like every other aspect of divorce settlements, custody is most often settled by agreement. Specifically, legal custody is usually accorded by agreement to the mother, since in most families, the mother is still the primary child raiser both before and after the divorce.[3] A good agreement will spell out a regular visitation schedule and the responsibilities of each of the parents (see Chapter 15). Ordinarily, unless the parents' agreement is found by the judge to be against the best interests of the child, the agreement will be adopted and made the judgment of the court.

If the parents cannot agree, the divorce or family court will gather information and make a decision. Both parents are asked to testify about their relationship with the child, and each is allowed to present witnesses. Depending on the age of the child, the child may be interviewed, either in open court or privately, by the judge or a child advocate. (In many states, a child age fourteen or older will have the right to decide with which parent to live, but younger children may or may not be asked their preference.) In some cases, the judge will ask a social worker to investigate by talking with the family and friends, to avoid the more formal court setting. Once all the evidence is gathered, the judge makes a decision based upon the best interests of the child.

The court's order may be temporary (if there is an ongoing divorce) or final (if the divorce or separation is being granted). Even a final order, however, may later be reopened by either parent if there is a change in circumstances.

MEN, WOMEN AND CUSTODY

Many people believe that family courts routinely favor mothers over fathers in custody disputes, and always have. In fact, this is true neither today nor historically. While it is true that women become the primary custodians of children after a divorce about 90 percent of the time, this is due not to court favoritism but to the fact that men generally don't seek custody. Court statistics show that when men do request custody, they tend to win at least as often as women.[4]

For most of the history of this country, in fact, custody of children upon separation or divorce was viewed as the automatic right of their father unless he could be shown to be clearly unfit.[5] This was because he was considered the head of the household, with a property right to the labor of the children. Toward the end of the 1800s, however, as the industrial revolution and the beginning of compulsory education made child labor less valuable, custody awards to women became more common.

As property interests began to give way to concern for child welfare, a new doctrine began to emerge in the early 1900s that "a child of tender years" would be better off with the mother. This soon gave way to what is still the law in every state: that custody should be decided based upon "the best interests of the child." While judges did commonly choose the mother in contested cases, it's unclear whether that was due to stereotyped ideas about sex roles or to the fact that women were most commonly the actual primary caretakers of the children both during the marriage and after the separation.

Today states vary in their guidelines for determining what is in the best interests of the child. At least two-thirds have formally rejected the old "child of tender years" rule, but a small minority will refer to it in deciding upon the child's best interests.[6] When it is used at all, it is generally only in the limited sense of upholding a custody award to a mother who acted as the homemaker and child raiser during the marriage. In no state is it interpreted to mean that men cannot be fit custodians for a child or that fathers who have been primary caretakers of the child in the past should not be considered in the same light as mothers who've had that responsibility.

Among the remaining majority of states, exact standards for determining what is in the best interests of the child differ. A great deal is left to the discretion of the individual judges who hear the cases, with mixed results. Although it's probably still true that there are some judges who favor traditional sex roles, that mind set is as likely to work against a working mother as for her. Such a judge may feel that a woman who works outside the home is a neglectful mother but that a man with a demanding job is a responsible father. Particularly if the father has a new wife (or even his mother) willing to care for the children on a daily basis, the judge may conclude that this is better than custody by the children's own working mother. The traditional social roles of male provider/female caretaker are left intact, but the women who provide the care are treated as interchangeable for one another.

The real catch-22, of course, is that with alimony almost extinct today and child support levels unrealistically low, most divorced mothers simply can't afford not to work. And, in fact, a divorced mother may suffer in a custody dispute if (as it usually is) her income is lower than her ex-husband's. A recent and controversial trend in some states allows consideration of the economic status of the parties and their ability to provide for the children.[7] This is a serious departure from the basic concept that child custody should go to the parent best fit to care for the child, with child support providing for the child's financial security.

JOINT CUSTODY

Joint custody, a recent and growing trend in divorce cases, might be a great idea in an ideal world, but it can create serious problems in the real world. This is because, legally speaking, it divides only the decision-making rights of parenting, while actual shared parenting responsibilities may or may not follow. If imposed in a case where one parent (generally the mother) will actually be providing most of the care for the children, it can result in continuing conflict. As already noted, the stability of custody arrangements, the child support levels and the decision-making power of the true custodial parent may all be threatened when legal custody doesn't reflect the actual caretaking arrangements.

Additionally, joint custody may open up a Pandora's box of potential arguments. Sadly, parents who couldn't agree during a marriage will often continue to argue after a divorce. The children may be caught in the middle, mere pawns in the struggles over where they should live or go to school, what rules to obey, even what medical care to seek.

It should be stressed, however, that joint custody does work well for some families. If two parents truly have been equally involved in child raising during the marriage and have unusual communication and conflict-resolution skills, they may wish to continue sharing parenting responsibilities on an equal basis after the divorce. In this case, joint custody can be a good way for them to share decision-making rights. Alternatively, they may prefer to both stay involved with the children but avoid potential decision-making conflicts by agreeing to legal custody by one parent, with extended visitation by the other.

Until recently, joint custody was viewed with caution, as an exceptional arrangement suitable only for parents with unusual co-parenting skills. In 1979, only six states had provisions specifically allowing joint custody. In recent years, however, that number has grown to at least thirty states, and more joint custody legislation is introduced each year.[8]

Some of these statutes simply allow joint custody as an option if both parents agree and the best interests of the child will be served by upholding the agreement. This type of legislation is basically reasonable and fair, in that it allows parents with a commitment to shared parenting to share decision-making responsibilities also.

Unfortunately, much of the new joint custody legislation goes far beyond simply allowing committed parents to agree to joint custody. In many states with joint custody statutes, judges have the power to order joint custody even when the parties do not agree to it. In some of these states, there is even a legal assumption that joint custody is the preferred arrangement unless it can be proven detrimental to the children. Since it's difficult to prove in advance that a new arrangement will be detrimental, joint custody may be imposed just because there's no proof one way or the other.

In some states judges are required to explain their reasoning in writing if joint custody is not ordered, but they need not provide any explanation if it is. There is a danger, then, that joint custody may be the easiest choice for a busy judge, even when it is not in the children's best interests.

Finally, in some states a parent may even risk losing custody altogether for opposing joint custody, however valid the objections, because of so-called friendly parent provisions. These state that in custody disputes the judge should favor the parent who shows the greatest willingness to provide access to the child by the other parent. Shockingly, no clear exceptions are provided, even in cases in which the other parent is suspected or known to be abusive.

THE PRIMARY CARETAKER STANDARD

A far more practical and healthy trend is developing in states that use what's called the *primary caretaker standard.*[9] These states, while rejecting the sexist notion that the primary caretaker in every family must necessarily be the mother, nonetheless affirm the importance of continuity of care within the family. If the mother provided the children with most of the care during the marriage and is not unfit, the court will presume that she should be the one to continue as their custodian after the divorce. If instead the father had fulfilled that role, he would, of course, be entitled to the same presumption. Joint custody would presumably be appropriate only in those cases in which child raising responsibilities had truly been shared equally during the marriage.

This rule has several important advantages. First, it affirms and fosters a child's legitimate needs for nurturance and continuity of care. It also affirms the roles of both parents by allowing them to continue with more or less the same division of labor as before the divorce. Finally, it avoids sex bias by not making assumptions about who was the primary caretaker and who was the primary wage earner during the marriage.

HOW CUSTODY STANDARDS AFFECT YOU

The important question, of course, is how all this affects your family. It certainly means that you must not take custody for granted but should be prepared to demonstrate actively your fitness as a custodial parent. It does not mean, however, that you should panic or despair over a possible custody conflict.

You needn't assume, first of all, that the children's father will seek custody or even joint custody. As already noted, most don't. Even if your husband has said he will seek custody, it's quite possible he won't follow through. Many men say this initially, either in anger at their wives or out of fear of losing contact with their children. Later, when things calm down, they often decide that a more traditional custody arrangement will better serve the family's needs.

You should also be aware that, despite the trends discussed here, most judges are still firmly committed to deciding custody based upon the best interests of the child. As a general rule, this still means preserving the continuity of care to the children as much as possible. If you've cared for the children in the past and relate to them well, you're in a good position to show that you should be the one to continue as their legal custodian.

Your first step in avoiding a custody problem is to learn about the specific laws in your state and the court trends in your area that may affect your case. The *only* sure way to do this is to consult with a capable lawyer, hired by you and with experience in child custody cases.

This cannot be stressed strongly enough. You can have your child support case handled by an OCSE worker or district attorney, but for child custody matters, you need the advice and help of an experienced, independent attorney.

Your lawyer will help you by defending a child custody action if needed, of course, but even more important, by advising you on how to avoid one. To start you thinking, here are a few guidelines that many attorneys feel are helpful in avoiding custody disputes. Since each is only a general rule, however, you should check directly with your lawyer to see which suggestions are suitable to your particular case.

The family least likely to experience a custody battle (or, for that matter, conflicts over support, property *or* custody) is the family in which both parents are sincerely concerned about the children's welfare and are able to communicate reasonably well with each other. Obviously you can't create that atmosphere singlehandedly, but you can do a great deal to help make it possible. In conversations with the children's father, try to avoid focusing on anger over the divorce but emphasize instead your shared concern for the children. Try to encourage a positive relationship and regular visitation between the children and their father, and to speak well of him in their presence.

Your efforts will be good for the children, of course, and may also have more immediate practical benefits. The open communication and sense of involvement in the family may well encourage the children's father to be more generous and cooperative in resolving custody and support matters. It will also place you in a positive light as a concerned mother and fair-minded person should any conflicts arise and be reported to a judge.

At the same time, it's a good idea to document quietly all you do to care for the children, whether you are now their legal custodian or are still negotiating custody. One smart practice is to keep a brief, matter-of-fact diary concerning child care. At the end of each day, write down where the children were during the day, how much time you spent with them and what you did together or for them (such as shopping, cooking, school visits and so on). If they visited with their father, write down how they reacted to the visit. If their father was supposed to visit them and did not, record this fact and how it appeared to affect the children. This diary will be your record if it's later claimed in a custody hearing either that you are not spending time with the children or that their father is spending more time with them than he really is.

If you are caring for the children and working outside the home, be certain that you've made adequate child care arrangements. Although this is often hard to do, especially on short notice or if your life is in divorce upheaval, it's crucial. It's important for your children's immediate safety and welfare, of course, but also as a way of demonstrating that you are a suitable custodian. Even a brief disruption in suitable child care arrangements can be damaging evidence in a custody hearing, so it's best to be very careful.

Similarly, it's generally helpful not to agree to even a temporary disruption of your day-to-day physical custody of the children. This is because continuity of care is one of the strongest factors you have going for you in any custody contest. Judges are quite understandably reluctant to disturb any child care arrangement that seems to be working, so legal custody in disputed cases often goes to the parent who has had physical custody since separation and at the time of the hearing.

Frequently a woman who has been the children's primary caretaker for years will, at divorce time, ask the children's father or some other relative or friend to care for the children for a few months while she gets settled. This may seem like a sensible move at the time, but it can create problems later. A judge may interpret this action as showing a lack of closeness with the children or ambivalence about wanting custody, or may simply feel the children have adjusted to the new situation and should therefore be left where they are.

All this puts a lot of pressure on you at a difficult time, of course. If possible, draw on whatever support system you have —or can create—for help. Keep the children living with you, but tap your parents, siblings and friends to help with their care. If you know other single mothers, perhaps from a social or support group, you could trade baby-sitting with them. Remember that this is really only for a relatively short period of time as you reorder your life after the divorce, and that it's for the children's good as well as your own. Everyone needs help sometime, and you'll have plenty of chances to return the favors later.

If you are faced with a custody request by the children's father, consult your attorney about the best strategy. Each case is quite different, and there's no set response that will be right for all. For example, a suggestion of joint custody by a father who'd been actively involved in child raising in the past might be quite reasonable, and you'd probably want to consider it (if you could agree on division of duties and support). That same suggestion from a father who'd been less involved with child care in the past, but who seemed sincere, might be more problematic. One reasonable response might be a proposal for a trial period of shared responsibility, with legal custody assigned to you during the trial period. But again, there are many factors you'd want to consider and discuss with your lawyer before making *any* agreement.

You might be faced with a custody request that is less than sincere. Many divorce lawyers report that men who are angry about a divorce may respond at least initially with a threat to seek custody. Similarly, some men respond to a child support collection action with a retaliatory change-of-custody action. At divorce time or later, custody may be used as a bargaining chip: that is, you withdraw your claim for support or shared property, and I'll withdraw my claim for custody.

Lawyers respond to these harsh tactics with a variety of strategies, such as proposing a cooling-off period before addressing the custody issue, reasoning, cajoling or even calling the bluff. You can help by being fair but firm. Point out your children's right to continuity of care and continued support, and resist attempts to pressure you into accepting less than what's fair.

At the same time, stay civil and try to avoid getting caught up in an ugly, angry fight. Above all (and this is hard under pressure), try to keep your children from being caught in the middle. Don't criticize their father in front of them or try to prevent visitation. Tempting as it may be to fight fire with fire, it can only worsen the acrimony, confuse and upset your children and quite possibly hurt your chances before a judge.

Custody is a serious issue, but it need not be a frightening one. Most mothers, having cared for the children before the divorce, do continue as their custodian afterward. Most fathers, at least by the time of the actual divorce decree, agree to or even request this arrangement. Finally, most judges, if asked to decide custody, do try to be fair and consider what has worked well in the past.

New trends in custody don't necessarily mean that your experience and commitment to the children will be ignored. You may, however, have to work a little harder to document and demonstrate it.

14

Keeping Your Family Safe

Physical violence against family members—by men against women and by parents against children—is rampant in our society.[1] Sexual abuse of children by fathers, stepfathers and other male relatives is also shockingly common.[2] If these are problems in your family, you and your children are not alone.

By separating from an abusive spouse, you have taken an important step in keeping your family safe. It probably wasn't easy to do, and it took a lot of strength on your part. Because expressions of power and control are part of abusive behavior, you may have been threatened: "If you leave, I'll find you and kill you." "You'll never get a penny, and you and the kids will spend your lives on welfare." "I'll take Susie and you'll never see her again. I'm her father, and I won't have you 'protecting' her from me."

Many of those threats were probably just threats. Still, it makes sense to guard against them. Violence and abuse don't just disappear because a marriage ends or a living situation changes. Sometimes it even gets worse as the abuser struggles to regain control. Or, possibly, it may appear to get better, but only as the abuser tries to persuade you to come back or to allow him extended unsupervised visitation with the children. That kind of temporary improvement more likely represents a change of tactics than a true change of heart.

It's not easy to protect yourself and your children against abusive behavior, but it can be done. The inner strength that allowed you to separate and begin again on your own will also help you take action to protect your family now.

FIGHTING ABUSIVE BEHAVIOR

Family violence, including child sexual abuse, is a crime both different from and more shocking than any other type of crime. It is a betrayal and a violation by someone who claims to love you (and perhaps on some level does) and whom you probably once loved (and perhaps still do). It's only natural to find yourself torn by wishful thinking that the violence will go away on its own. It's also natural to want to stop it but to be hesitant—out of fear or out of love—to do anything that might hurt the abuser.

Unfortunately, abusive behavior rarely does go away on its own, and you can't make it go away with heartfelt pleas or an appeal to fairness. Keep in mind that a tendency toward violence is deeply ingrained. You didn't cause it. You can't cure it, and you can't, by yourself, control it. You can, however, take positive steps to protect yourself and your children from it.

There are two basic ways to protect your family, and each has its advantages and disadvantages. One option is to remove yourself and your children completely from the abuser's reach—by fleeing to another community or even another state, then keeping your new location secret. This is a very effective method of avoiding violent contact, but it also means that positive relating, if any, between parent and child will also end. It may also be very difficult to collect any child support.

Alternatively, you can maintain family contact, but in a manner tightly controlled by persons in higher authority. In effect, with the help of the legal system, you're saying, "Okay, you can see the kids and continue in your role as a parent, but if you're violent toward me or them, you'll suffer some consequences. You may lose your right to see them anymore or you may get arrested, or both." The intent, of course, is not to land the abuser in jail or to cut off the parent-child relationship but to prevent violent acts by making it clear they won't be permitted.

Possibly neither of these two routes will seem quite right for your family. You might find the first option too extreme in cutting off all contact but the second too risky due to the continuing regular contact. If so, it might make sense to combine parts of both into a plan that fits your family needs. For example, you might move to another state but not keep your location secret. Instead, you could seek sole custody with strictly limited visitation. Due to the distance, much of that visitation might be carried out through the much safer medium of cards and phone calls.

What kind of protection you seek is a decision only you can make. A great deal will depend on your own family dynamics —whether the violence is frequent or occasional, how severe it is, how much the children are affected and whether there are any positive aspects to the parent-child relationship worth trying to salvage. You'll also want to find out from local sources such as your lawyer or a battered women's group how effective court and law-enforcement protection in the area tend to be.

There's a strong impulse in family violence cases to avoid even trying to collect child support. Some people feel it's best to get as far away as possible and to cut all family ties with an abuser. They fear that child support will tend to keep the lines of communication and contact open—and, in fact, this is often true. For this reason, some women who've been battered or seen their children abused feel very strongly that they will never seek support from the abuser.[3]

While this is the best choice for some families, it's certainly not right for all. For one thing, money is money, and children need to eat. If you truly need child support, it might be necessary to take some carefully limited risks.

It may also not be practical or desirable in your case to cut off contact altogether. If so, it could actually be more dangerous to appear to reward violence by not seeking support. Suppose, for example, your husband threatens violence at the first suggestion that you'll be seeking child support. If you then agree not to seek support, he may conclude that violence is a good method for getting his own way. As you face other possible disagreements—over custody, visitation, property matters, even whether to renew your relationship or give in to his sexual demands—you may find yourself in a threatening atmosphere of increasing violence and intimidation.

Perhaps the only really helpful general rule is to choose your course and then follow it vigorously and completely. If you decide to hide, hide effectively; don't stay with a friend down the street and let the children play out front. If you have provisions in a divorce agreement designed to protect the children during visitation, consult your lawyer at the very first violation. And if you get a protective order that says your abusive husband will be arrested if he tries to enter your home, call the police if he's jimmying the front door lock.

Keep in mind that even violent people don't behave violently just because they're angry. With very few exceptions, they do so when they are angry *and* they think they can get away with it. For example, the man who blows up in your kitchen over burned toast will probably not blow up at a police officer who gives him a speeding ticket. He may be angry—far angrier than he was over the toast—but, eyeing the officer's badge and gun, he'll probably nod and respond politely.

Your goal, then, whether you decide to flee secretly or to use the legal system to protect yourself, is to guarantee that the abuser can't engage in violent acts toward you or the children and get away with it. The rest of this chapter will describe specific tools to help you do that. We'll also discuss how child support enforcement will be affected by your choices.

You can get other helpful information, emotional support and possibly even emergency shelter from a battered women's service group in your area, or in your new area if you move. To find one, just call telephone information locally or, if you live in a rural area, in the nearest city. The service group can also help put you in touch with lawyers and others trained to help women get protection from the legal system.

POLICE PROTECTION

It is a crime in every state to hit or beat another person, whether or not that person is a family member. Your family is entitled to police protection from battering, if necessary by having the batterer arrested and removed from the home. Anytime you or a child is in immediate physical danger, it's a good idea to call the police for protection.

Studies show that the police action most effective in preventing future violence is an immediate arrest.[4] Even if the abuser is soon released on bail, the arrest delivers a strong message that violent behavior is not allowed and carries serious penalties.

It is not always possible, however, to have the batterer arrested. One reason is a common limitation on police arrest powers. Hitting or beating alone *(battery)* and threatening to hit or beat *(assault)* are among the class of crime considered least serious *(misdemeanors).* Generally a police officer cannot make an arrest for a misdemeanor unless it is committed in the officer's presence. Since the beating generally stops when the police come to the door, no arrest may result.

Assault or battery with a weapon or with the intent to kill or rape is considered a more serious crime (a *felony*). In most states, the weapon need not be a gun or a knife; it could be anything likely to injure someone, such as a table fork, a telephone receiver or a book. A few states will even consider a strong man's fists a weapon, so that it would be a felony for him to strike with his fists.

An officer can arrest—and in fact has a legal duty to arrest—whenever there is "probable cause" to believe a felony has been committed. Probable cause means just what it sounds like: that there's cause to believe the event probably happened. So if you explain to the officer that your husband beat you with his fists and his shoe, and you're obviously bruised or cut, the officer would have probable cause to make an arrest.

Some police departments handle domestic violence cases

seriously and appropriately, making arrests when it is possible and issuing stern warnings when it is not. Others are less responsive and therefore less effective. Your local battered women's group can probably give you tips about your area police.

Police protection has no direct effect on the child support process. Indirectly, effective protection can help by creating a safer environment for resolving conflicts.

It is also a crime to abuse a child sexually, but pursuing a criminal remedy for this may be more problematic. A sexual abuse case can be difficult to document, and the child may have to be questioned repeatedly. Also, because children don't understand that they're not responsible for sexual abuse, the child may worry that "Daddy is going to jail because of something I did with him."

Certainly there are times when an arrest for child sexual abuse is appropriate, but it's often a complicated decision. Before you call the police (other than to stop an immediate threat of rape or sexual assault), it's a good idea to consult with a lawyer and a mental health counselor experienced in abuse cases. The lawyer will help you explore your options for protection, while the mental health counselor will help reassure your child. If your child needs a physical exam because of the abuse, the lawyer or counselor can also help arrange that. Both will help you make sound decisions and restore a safer family atmosphere.

There's another reason it's important to get this assistance right away. Whatever you eventually decide to do—whether it's to seek an arrest, a protective order or sole custody with limited or no visitation—you'll need to be sure the abuse is well documented. Without a supporting medical or psychological report, you would probably have difficulty convincing a judge of the seriousness of the problem. By working with a lawyer and a counselor, you'll be better able to get the documentation you need to protect your child.

It's essential that you act as quickly as possible once you discover or suspect that sexual abuse is occurring. If you need help taking immediate action, contact a rape crisis center or a battered women's hot line. Even if you have no money to pay, the people there can arrange for a counselor to see your child right away and will probably be able to recommend a lawyer or legal assistance program to meet your family needs.

PROTECTIVE ORDERS

In many states (thanks to the lobbying efforts of battered women's advocates), you can now get extended police and court protection through the use of domestic violence protective orders. Details vary by state, but here's a general idea of how they work. To get information specific to your area, ask your local battered women's service group, your local police or at the courthouse nearest you.

To get a protective order, you would fill out a simple petition at the court assigned to hear those cases. You would then go before a judge to testify about the violence and abuse occurring against you or the children. If you can bring any proof, it's very helpful. Some women will have a friend take color photographs of cuts and bruises as soon as they happen and will get copies of medical reports from any clinic they visit for treatment of injuries. If you have any witnesses—friends or neighbors who have seen the violent behavior—bring them too. Finally, it's a good idea (although not legally required) to bring a lawyer or other advocate to help you present your case.

The judge, after hearing your evidence, would have the power to issue a temporary order to protect you. The order might be quite limited (perhaps merely ordering the abuser to refrain from hitting, threatening or harassing you or the children) or more extensive (for example, ordering the abuser to leave the family home, and ordering the police or sheriff to arrest and hold him while you have the locks changed).

Note that this hearing, unlike almost every other kind of legal hearing, is one-sided. You're there, but the person you're complaining about (the defendant) isn't. This is because it's an emergency. The defendant will have his chance to answer, however. Within a week or two, a second hearing will be set, and both of you will have a chance to come in and be heard. *Be sure to attend this second hearing, with a lawyer if possible.* Generally that first emergency order lasts only until the second hearing, and if you're not there to describe the violence and ask for an extension of the order, you'll lose your protection.

What exactly does a protective order do for you? First, it shows the abuser that you're serious about stopping the abuse and will take legal action if necessary. In some cases, it can give you immediate police assistance in getting an abuser to leave (even if the residence is in his name) or in leaving with the children yourself. It also lets the abuser know that his actions are not permitted by the legal authorities—in effect, that he's being watched.

Your having a protective order may also give the police extra arrest powers if the order is later violated. Here's why. As you just learned, it's a general rule that police can't arrest for a simple assault or battery unless it occurred in their presence. In most states with protective order laws, however, the police have a duty to arrest if there's probable cause to believe a protective order has been violated. This is true even if the offense would not otherwise be considered a felony and even if it wasn't committed in the officer's presence. If the order said the abuser musn't come near you, for example, he could be arrested for following you home from work or trying to enter the apartment.

Protective orders are often helpful in child sexual abuse cases. Once again, though, it's best to consult an experienced attorney to discuss all your options.

In some states, protective orders may contain provisions for temporary custody of the children and for temporary alimony and/or child support.

SUPERVISED VISITATION

If there are positive aspects to the relationship between the children and the noncustodial parent, you may be wondering whether visitation will be possible and if it's a good idea. Once again, that's a big decision, and you'll probably want help thinking it through. A lot will depend on how severe the abuse was, how long ago it happened, whether the noncustodial parent has sought counseling or other help and how the children themselves feel. If the noncustodial parent is violent and abusive now —even if the abuse has so far been directed toward you and not the children—it's really not safe to trust him with the children. Certainly he's not a good influence on them.[5] Yet people do change, and not everyone who's abusive once remains abusive forever.

If you do consider agreeing to visitation (or if the judge orders visitation despite your concerns and objections), you'll want to seek arrangements that are carefully structured and preferably supervised. Your lawyer can help you work out exact details, but it may be helpful to know about some possible options. None is safe with a strong, actively violent man, but each can be helpful for maintaining a sense of structure and control with a noncustodial parent who's been abusive in the past but shows a willingness to avoid abusive behavior now.

You might, for example, agree to brief daytime visits in public areas only, such as a playground or park near your home. Or, if you have family in the area, perhaps arrangements could be made for the noncustodial parent to visit the children at your parents' or other relatives' house. (Visitation at his parents' house is not good protection, since they may not believe he's potentially abusive and may do little to supervise.)

Every state has a social service department assigned to protect children from abuse, and you could enlist its aid in supervising visitation. If the staff agrees there's a need, the services will probably be free. They may also offer free or low-cost counseling if needed.

You should understand, however, that the social service agency will be there primarily to serve and protect the children, not to respond to your service requests. This means that if you and they have different opinions about what's right for the children, they're likely to follow their judgment rather than yours. They might also report their opinions—about the children and about both parents—to the judge.

Obviously there are many factors to consider before agreeing to any supervised visitation plan. It's no cure-all, even when the noncustodial parent is reasonably cooperative. If he's actively resistant to the plan, it could spell future danger. Yet for some families, it makes sense as a way to maintain what's good in a parent-child bond while guarding against the bad.

Supervised visitation doesn't affect support collection directly, but it's sometimes difficult to keep the two from getting mixed up together. You could take the noncustodial parent back to court for violating the safety rules of the visitation agreement, for example, and he could respond by withholding his next support payment.

As much as possible, it's helpful to keep the two issues separate. If you can get a wage assignment and have support sent directly from the noncustodial parent's employer, for example, there will be less chance that support will be used as a weapon or a bargaining wedge. That will leave you free to focus on the most important goal: keeping your children as safe as possible.

Before you agree to anything or make any decisions about supervised visitation, talk it over carefully with your lawyer. Discuss what's happened in the past, what the terms of any visitation agreement might be and what will happen if the terms are violated. You probably already have a good sense of your own family needs, but you need an equally clear understanding of your options.

KEEPING YOUR LOCATION SECRET

If the violence against you or the children has been severe, you may wish to consider leaving secretly and keeping your new location secret. This option, although it is not right for every family, has allowed many formerly battered women and their children to make a fresh start.

Most medium- or large-sized cities and even some smaller communities have emergency protective shelters for women and children escaping from family violence and abuse. They tend to be crowded but friendly, with dedicated staffers who understand (and often have been in) situations like your own. They can help you find housing and a job if necessary, as well as ease the transition for you and the children by offering emotional support and counseling. Shelter locations are kept secret for your protection, but you can get in touch with them by phone. Most shelters are free or very low cost to families in need.

You should know that many shelters struggle with problems of inadequate funding and are often filled to capacity. If you call a shelter and it's filled, ask where else you might call, and keep trying. If you're thinking about moving out of state, you could ask your local shelter to help you make contact with shelters in the new community.

As noted, it's difficult to keep your location secret and collect child support. The traditional rule in lawsuits is that the addresses of both parties must be on record, and many judges don't understand the importance of keeping an address hidden from an abuser. Also, some judges seem to feel that any parent who supports has a right to see the child regularly, no matter what the circumstances. Of course, attitudes vary, and your lawyer will probably have a sense about your chances in the local courts.

There is also the logical problem of where to have support checks sent. Fortunately, many courts have a procedure for noncustodial parents to pay through a clearinghouse (either connected to the court itself or through the local OCSE office). Although the real purpose of these clearinghouses is to simplify recordkeeping on child support payments, they can help by putting a buffer between you and the abuser.

In general, though, it is extremely difficult to live near a violent noncustodial parent, collect support and successfully keep your location secret. A somewhat more workable way to stay safely hidden is to move out of state and seek support collection through URESA. Since URESA courts do not ordinarily handle custody and visitation matters, there's little chance that visitation will be ordered. Also, most URESA offices will allow you to file your case without stating your address if there is danger to your family in releasing it. Finally, since you're in another state, it will be more difficult and less tempting to try to find you, even if the abuser is angered by an order to pay child support.

Fleeing to another state can occasionally create custody problems if it's not clear to a court deciding custody why you left the state. For this reason, you should consult with a lawyer *before* you leave the state, if possible. If that's not possible—if you and the children are in immediate danger and can't wait for legal advice—then at least be sure to contact a lawyer as soon as you arrive in the new state.

If you are already involved in a divorce or legal separation, you should be doubly sure to consult with your lawyer before you flee. Because the case is already open, the judge has the power to decide custody at any time. The last thing you want is for that decision to be made in your absence, with your lawyer not certain where you are, why you left or what you want done. To protect your family safety and stability, stay in touch and follow your lawyer's advice.

EMOTIONAL SUPPORT

Battering and abuse are frightening, painful and emotionally draining. Whether you hide, leave the community or stay and get protection, you'll need all the emotional support you can get. Fortunately there are several ways to find supportive people who will understand your feelings and help you work them through.

As hard as you've worked to get out of a dangerous situation, you have every reason to think of yourself as a strong person. You may want to put that time behind you and to encourage your children to do the same. Thinking about past experiences may seem like backtracking and talking about them with others a sign of weakness.

In fact, it's a sign of strength and growth, not of weakness, to reach out to others who understand your situation. While you were in a day-to-day dangerous situation, it probably took all your energy just to react and plan. To really let it register how scary it all felt would seem too overwhelming. Now that you're safer, you can begin to express those feelings and to learn from your experiences as you talk with others about them.

Your children, too, will have strong feelings and many adjustments to make. You can get direct help in dealing with any problems they might have, and you can also help them indirectly just by taking care of your own emotional needs.

One good place to get emotional support we've already mentioned: battered women's shelters and service groups. Many offer support groups for women who've left abusive family situations. They may also have professional counselors who can help. Their services are generally free or very low cost.

Community health centers may also offer low-cost counseling or support groups. If you're interested in counseling for your children or for yourself and the children as a family, community health centers are a good place to check. You might also ask the guidance counselor or school psychologist at your children's school.

Perhaps you're concerned about your own parenting skills. Violence breeds violence, and there may be times when you get so frustrated you feel like lashing out at the children. You may have caught yourself hitting a child angrily and fear you'll do so again. If so, you owe it to yourself and your children to get help.

Private and family counseling can help you improve your relationship with the children and avoid any possible violence, but there's also an excellent self-help support group. Known as Parents Anonymous, it has chapters all over the country. It is made up of concerned parents like you, many of whom were at one time the victims of violence, as children or adults, and all of whom, as parents, have had to learn to overcome their own violent impulses.

Perhaps someone in your family is or was a heavy drinker. There's a unique sort of tangled emotional web in families affected by alcohol abuse that no one understands quite like someone who's been there. That can make you feel very alone as you try to sort through your feelings, but it needn't. There's a wonderful support group of people who've lived and in many cases still live in families affected by alcohol abuse. Known as Al-Anon Family Groups, this self-help organization has groups all across the country.

There's a lovely passage you may hear read aloud if you go to a meeting of a self-help support group. "Whatever your problems, there are those among us who have had them, too. If you try to keep an open mind, you will find help. You'll learn that there is no situation too difficult to be bettered, and no unhappiness too great to be lessened."[6]

Now that's help and wisdom we could all use at times.

15

Structuring Your Agreement

As you and the noncustodial parent negotiate, there will be many important decisions to make. You'll need to make workable arrangements for the children's custody, visitation, support, education, health care and safety. If you are also ending a marriage through divorce or legal separation, other matters, such as property division, alimony and responsibility for debts, will have to be decided. Many of the decisions you make will affect your life for the next several years—not only emotionally but also in terms of financial security and opportunity. In fact, your written separation agreement will probably be the most important financial transaction you ever make.

For every provision of your agreement, you should think carefully about what its practical effect will be. Of course, you hope that everything will happen as planned, but try to search out possible weaknesses in your agreement by imagining what could go wrong.

For example, hurried lawyers often try to save time on visitation arrangements by putting a clause in the final agreement allowing "reasonable visitation." This may be fine if you know that the noncustodial parent is invariably considerate and has a view similar to yours of what "reasonable visitation" means. Few divorcing parents get along so well, however, and for most families, vague wording invites trouble. A better approach is to state clearly when and how visitation will take place (e.g., Saturday overnights each weekend, with twenty-four hours' notice in case of cancelation).

This kind of practical thinking should also be used to evaluate your financial future under any proposed agreement. Suppose, for example, you've been the primary homemaker in the family and it's suggested that you live in the family home with the children until they're eighteen, then sell the house and split the proceeds. Is this really adequate? Will you be financially ready at that time to make other suitable living arrangements? And what about the children—will this make it impossible for them to live at home and attend a local school, or to come home for summers and vacations? If these are problems in your case, you would probably want to argue strongly against the proposed sale of the house.

Finally, most separation agreements have significant tax effects. In order to evaluate financial and property provisions, it's essential to know exactly what you'll be getting in after-tax dollars and what taxes you'll be responsible for paying. What looks like a good agreement on its face may in fact be a terrible one once you've finished paying Uncle Sam's share.

Evaluating tax consequences is quite technical, and you can't be expected to do it alone. Tax regulations are often complicated, and there are new laws to consider each year. In fact, even many divorce lawyers do not have the technical expertise to evaluate tax effects. What they do—and what you should ask about having your lawyer do—is to call in a good tax accountant. It's a small investment to make in your financial future and could save you literally thousands of dollars in unexpected tax bills.

Divorce and separation agreements should cover each of the following areas. For each topic, we'll look at some specific matters you'll want to consider and discuss with your lawyer.

CHILD CUSTODY AND VISITATION

Your agreement should clearly state who has legal custody of the child or children. Remember that you won't automatically be the legal custodian just because you're the one caring for the children most of the time. You need to specify it in the agreement. This is important because it establishes your right to make such decisions as where you and the children will live, where they'll go to school and so on (see Chapter 13).

If you decide instead to specify joint legal custody, it might be a good idea to carve out certain areas in which each of the parents will make the final decisions. For example, if you are caring for the children during the week, the agreement might state that you have the responsibility for deciding what after-school activities the children may attend. Saturday activities might reasonably be decided by the parent who cares for the children on Saturdays. By dividing decision-making authority, you avoid possible conflict and disagreement.

This portion of your agreement should also state who will be caring for the children when, and what the arrangements for visitation will be. Keep the agreement as simple and regular as possible so you can plan ahead. As you plan for weekends, holidays and school vacations, be sure to keep in mind your own need to spend some of these more restful times with the children. Some custodial parents agree to having the children spend so much weekend and holiday time with the noncustodial parent that they end up only seeing the children during the week, when time is limited and tempers are short.

If you feel it's important to your children to see the noncustodial parent but fear he'll visit irregularly, stress your interest in regular visitation during negotiations. Ask to include a statement in the agreement that visitation is not merely a right but a responsibility and that the noncustodial parent promises to visit as agreed. Also, since you'll probably depend on those visitation periods in making your own plans, you might want to ask for a provision that the noncustodial parent will pay a set amount for alternate child care arrangements if he cancels on short notice. These provisions can't guarantee reliability, of course, but they may help. They're also a way of stressing the importance of the noncustodial parent's role in raising the children.

Alternatively, if you have concerns about the children's safety with the noncustodial parent, this would be the place to include restrictions about supervised visitation, not taking the children out-of-state, no overnights and so on (see Chapter 14). You might even want to include more common safety rules such as that both parents agree to require children to use seat belts, or will not leave young children home alone. Promises can be broken, of course, but they also may be taken seriously, particularly when they're made by mutual agreement.

If the provisions are not followed, you could go back to the judge handling your case and ask that the agreement be either enforced or modified to fit the new situation. For example, if the noncustodial parent promised to care for the children for a month in the summer and is not doing so, you could ask for extra child support to cover the added expense. If, on the other hand, he's failing to return the children reliably after daytime visitation, you could ask that he be allowed only to visit them in or near your home. You might or might not get this relief, but your case would be helped by the fact that you'd made a clear agreement of rights and responsibilities.

CHILD SUPPORT AND ALIMONY

Support provisions should clearly indicate what is alimony and what is child support, since each has different practical and tax effects (see Chapter 12). For each, it should be stated how much will be paid, how often and how long it will continue. Although alimony is generally presumed to end at remarriage or death and child support when the child reaches age eighteen, in most states, this can be changed by agreement.

Most people prefer to have child support (like alimony) paid year-round, even during vacations when the children are with the noncustodial parent. This is because many costs of raising children, such as maintaining a home large enough for them, will continue even when they're away on vacation. Your agreement should specify whether payments will continue when the children are with the noncustodial parent, to avoid a later dispute.

To help protect against inflation, it's a good idea to structure a regular cost-of-living increase into your agreement. A common method is to set basic sums for alimony and child support, then provide for regular increases based upon one of the following:

- a set percentage (e.g., 5 percent a year)
- raises in the noncustodial parent's income (e.g., support raised each year by a percentage equal to the percentage increase of the noncustodial parent's income, as shown on federal tax returns)
- government consumer price index figures

Talk to your lawyer about this, because states vary as to which types of cost-of-living provisions will be allowed and enforced. Generally speaking, escalation clauses based upon the consumer price index are most favored.

If you are concerned about whether support payments will be paid promptly and reliably, you might ask the noncustodial parent to agree to a wage assignment. Under a wage assignment, the noncustodial parent's employer would deduct support payments from each paycheck and send them directly to you.

Wage assignments (both voluntary and court-ordered) are becoming increasingly common, and many noncustodial parents find that it's actually a more convenient way to pay support. They feel that if they don't see the money they won't be tempted to spend it, and they'll probably miss it less. Just as with withholding taxes, it quickly becomes a matter of course.

EDUCATION AND CHILD CARE

If you are or will be working and have small children, you will have to make arrangements for day care. You may also have older children requiring after-school care or lessons, or perhaps attending a private or parochial school. If so, your agreement should provide for payment of these expenses.

Basically, there are two ways to do this. You can pay school and child care costs yourself but receive a higher child support payment to reflect the expense. Or you can structure into the agreement that the noncustodial parent will be responsible for paying certain tuition costs directly to the provider. One advantage of the latter method is that it avoids arguments over how the money is being spent. A disadvantage is that it can create conflicts with the school if there is a nonpayment problem.

College expenses are another important priority, and you should use the separation agreement to plan ahead for them. In most states, judges cannot order parents to provide children with the means for a college education if the parents don't agree to it. They will, however, allow and later enforce an agreement that you and the noncustodial parent make at divorce or separation time.

One common method is simply to include an agreement that the noncustodial parent will pay reasonable college tuition and living expenses. Unfortunately, this once again leaves open the question of what is reasonable. Worse yet, it may put your child in the middle if the noncustodial parent decides halfway through the school year that the tuition is unreasonable and stops paying.

Yet setting an exact sum can also create problems. Particularly if your children are young, it's difficult to predict how much a college education will cost when they reach college age. Still, you could make your best guess and then agree to a provision, for example, that the noncustodial parent will pay reasonable tuition and living expenses, and that any sum under $15,-000 a year will automatically be deemed reasonable.

Alternatively, you could agree on a school in your price range and specify that the noncustodial parent would pay reasonable tuition and living expenses in a sum not to exceed the amount charged at the time by University X. Your children would not have to attend University X, of course, but they would know their cost ceiling.

Finally, you might want to consider setting up a special savings account now for each child's future college expenses. Most banks offer special education accounts for this purpose, which allow you to put the money in trust for your child until he or she is eighteen. Because the interest income on the accounts is legally your child's rather than your own, any taxes on it would be at your child's tax rate, not yours. Since most children don't have enough income to pay taxes, that means it would effectively be tax-free. You could set up an account like this and, as part of the separation agreement, require the noncustodial parent to begin now to pay a certain amount into the fund each month as part of the child-support obligation.

Keep in mind that the noncustodial parent may, as years pass, take on new family obligations. Provisions in your divorce or separation agreement now can keep your child's education from being lost in the shuffle later.

HEALTH CARE

These days an unplanned health emergency can be financially disastrous. Every family needs the coverage of a good health insurance plan or health maintenance organization, and yours is no exception.

If the noncustodial parent is employed, quite likely his employer offers a group plan that can be used to cover the children. Additionally, if you were covered under the policy during your marriage, it may be possible to convert your coverage to individual coverage at the group rate. This is generally much less expensive than beginning a new individual policy, and you won't have to pass a physical exam to qualify.

Your separation agreement should state whether the noncustodial parent will be responsible for maintaining health insurance for you and/or the children. If so, it should also state that he will be responsible for all medical expenses. That way, when you take the children for medical care, you can indicate on forms that the noncustodial parent will be responsible for bill payment and have the bills sent directly to him. If the health care provider questions this procedure, you'll have the agreement to show that the noncustodial parent has accepted the legal responsibility for health care costs.

If possible, the agreement should specify that dental care, ophthalmology and optometry are also included in the noncustodial parent's responsibility to pay for health care. Additionally, if your family has or anticipates special needs such as orthodontia, psychological counseling or physical therapy, there should be a specific agreement about these. Courts vary as to whether they will consider these kinds of care ordinary medical expenses under a separation agreement, so it's best to avoid confusion by specifying in advance.

OTHER INSURANCE

Your children need the support of two parents. You can't protect them against the emotional loss if a parent dies, but you can and should protect them against the financial impact by maintaining life insurance.

If the noncustodial parent has a substantial life insurance policy through work, you could seek an assignment of the proceeds to you (or in trust to the children, payable to you). This should be included as a provision of your written separation agreement, but the noncustodial parent will also have to sign a form at work assigning the policy. You or your lawyer should follow up with a letter to the insurer notifying them of your agreement and requesting a letter indicating that (a) the policy has been properly assigned, and (b) it will not be terminated or reassigned to someone else without notice to you first. Finally, the separation agreement should state that the noncustodial parent will buy or maintain for your benefit a life insurance policy of equal value should that policy ever be terminated.

An even better protection is to own a life insurance policy on the noncustodial parent yourself. If the noncustodial parent now owns a life insurance policy, ownership (and responsibility for paying premiums) can be transferred to you. If it's an old policy, started several years ago, the premiums will probably be quite modest and may even be all or nearly all paid up. There may even be a present cash value to the policy.

Most important, your ownership of the policy will mean there's no danger that it will later be reassigned to someone else or terminated due to nonpayment or a request by the noncustodial parent. You'll never have to worry or ask a court for enforcement, and your children will be protected against future financial loss.

This is also an important time to review your own insurance needs and other protections for your children's future. Your children depend on your financially as well as emotionally, and you should have life insurance and an up-to-date will. You'll also need homeowner's or renter's insurance to protect your home and belongings. These probably won't go into the separation agreement, but they are just as important to your family's security. With all the changes you may be going through now, you need to be sure not to overlook your own insurance and other needs.

PROPERTY DIVISION

Dividing property fairly can be one of the most difficult tasks of a divorce agreement. Legal standards for making a division do exist, but they are at best an incomplete guide.

In many states, for example, the law says that there should be an *equitable division* of property. Basically this is just legalese for doing what's fair, based upon such factors as the length of the marriage, the contribution of each of the spouses during the marriage (including child raising and homemaking), the future earning power of each, who will be caring for the children and the arrangements for continuing support. Some states also allow consideration of who was at fault in causing the breakup.

Other states follow the *community property* rule. This means, in theory, that all property acquired during the marriage through the efforts of either spouse will be divided equally between the two spouses. Yet since many assets (such as a house, car or furniture) cannot conveniently be split in half, it is still necessary to make trade-offs and negotiate what is fair.

Perhaps the most important factor in negotiating a fair property division is knowing exactly what you are dividing. This means first making sure that all assets to be divided have been declared or discovered (see Chapter 11), then seeing that all major assets have been properly valued.

Suppose, for example, you were asked to trade your interest in the family business for your spouse's interest in the family home. Unless you knew exactly what each was worth, you couldn't possibly know if this was a reasonable trade.

For this reason, you may need to have major assets professionally appraised. A qualified business accountant can determine the worth of a family business, while an independent real estate appraiser will tell you the market value of houses or other property. Talk to your lawyer about this, particularly if your spouse is offering value estimates that you suspect may be inaccurate.

Your spouse will also probably hire an expert to appraise any major asset, but you can't rely safely on the figures of his appraiser alone. You'll need your own expert, paid by you, to really go through company books or real estate records to discover any telltale signs of undervaluation. This is particularly true if it's an asset that has been managed by your spouse in the past.

Tax effects are another extremely important part of negotiating a fair property division. Specifically, you should ask about the eventual payment of a capital gains tax on any property exchanged through the agreement.

The capital gains tax is a special tax the IRS imposes whenever property is sold or exchanged at a profit. Until recently, the capital gains tax on a major asset such as a house had to be paid at divorce time if the asset changed hands from one spouse to the other. Now, due to recent changes in federal tax law (the

Domestic Relations Tax Act of 1984), the entire tax will be paid later, when the asset is sold at a profit.

There's an important reason to think about capital gains tax now, even if there are no immediate plans to sell the house or other assets. If your husband offers you the house in exchange for other valuable property or rights, you and your lawyer need to remember while negotiating that it is a house with a tax liability.

For example, suppose the house is now worth $80,000, but the original purchase price was only $30,000. Depending upon your tax bracket, you could pay a capital gains tax of as high as $10,000 to the federal government, plus any capital gains tax your state might impose. You would probably have other expenses at that time, too, such as a mortgage balance owed to the bank, unpaid property taxes, cost of needed repairs and real estate sales costs. Thus by the time you finished paying taxes and other expenses, that "$80,000 house" might turn out to be worth only half that sum in real dollars.

This change in federal tax law is so new that many divorce lawyers haven't yet begun advising their clients to plan ahead for the capital gains tax. Worse yet, they may bargain as if it didn't exist—as if that "$80,000 house" really was worth just that. Because the tax is no longer paid right away (and because the case will be over for them when it's paid years later), both lawyers may overlook it completely. But if you're the one who's going to be paying it someday when you sell the house or other asset, you need to be sure it's not overlooked. Ask your lawyer directly if you will be responsible for future capital gains taxes and if that fact has been considered in negotiating the agreement.

An important, frequently ignored subject of property division is pension rights. In many families, pension rights in the name of the noncustodial parent are the most valuable asset the family owns. By law they are, in most cases, considered a part of the marital estate subject to division—but you need to be sure they aren't overlooked.

Basically, then, there are three essential rules to a fair property division: know what there is to be divided, know what it's worth and know what it's worth in after-tax dollars. This, combined with your lawyer's active advocacy, is your key to avoiding unfairness and unexpected financial hardship.

OTHER PROVISIONS

There are several other matters that a good divorce or separation agreement should address. If any of the following do not appear in an agreement prepared for your signature, check with your lawyer to find out why.

- A provision stating who will pay for *attorney fees.*
- An allocation of *responsibility for debts* already owed.
- A disclaimer of responsibility for *future debts* of the other spouse.
- A statement that *reconciliation* with your spouse will not automatically negate the agreement. (In most states, a single act of intercourse may be considered reconciliation, and you don't want to be seduced into giving up your rights under the agreement.)
- A provision that attorney fees for any *future actions* to enforce the agreement will be paid by the party not in compliance. (This protects you against the cost of enforcement if the noncustodial parent fails to support or otherwise live up to the agreement.)
- A warranty that there has been *full disclosure* of all income and assets of the parties. (This helps you to later reopen the case if you discover that assets were hidden from you.)
- A statement of who will take the federal income tax *dependency deduction* for the children. (By law, that right goes to their primary caretaker, unless specifically waived in writing.)
- A mutual *covenant to execute documents* necessary to put the agreement into effect (such as property deeds, stock transfers, insurance assignments, etc.).

- A mutual *waiver of inheritance rights* not specifically reserved in the agreement.
- A statement that the signing of the agreement is *voluntary and knowledgeable,* in that both parties understand it and are not under duress to sign.

Divorce is stressful, and negotiating a divorce agreement can be an added stress. Keep in mind, though, that your vigorous efforts can result in a fair agreement that will reduce your financial and even emotional stress for years to come.

As you review your divorce or separation agreement before signing, think carefully about the terms. For each provision, ask yourself the following questions:

- Is this provision clearly stated so that no one could misunderstand its meaning?
- Is it a provision I can live with financially and emotionally?
- Do I really understand the agreement fully, including its long-range practical, financial and tax effects?
- Is the total effect of the agreement fair and reasonable?

If you can answer yes to all these questions, congratulate yourself on a job well done. Your success in putting together a solid agreement will be a help to your family for years to come.

III

COLLECTING
OVERDUE SUPPORT

16

Documenting Nonpayment

Your child support order is, to look at it, an ordinary piece of paper. If you received your order a while ago and have since collected little or no support, it may seem as if it and some change will buy you a cup of coffee. That piece of paper alone won't make a noncustodial parent pay support, or get his employer to send you a portion of his paycheck, or send the sheriff out to seize and sell the nonsupporter's car. It is, however, an important tool that can make it possible for you to do all that and more. Your child support order establishes your legal right to collect a specified amount of support—but you'll have to do the footwork to enforce it if it's not obeyed.

Your first step in collecting is keeping accurate records of payment and nonpayment. If you're receiving nothing, of course, it won't take any fancy records to keep track of that. Yet many custodial parents receive occasional payments, don't keep track of them and then face a claim later in court from the noncustodial parent that he's been paying all along. If neither side has accurate records, the judge may be inclined to let bygones be bygones.

If you got your order through the OCSE, the URESA system or the criminal justice system, this probably won't be a problem for you. Each of these programs ordinarily arranges to have all payments made through them and to keep their own payment records. Some family courts have a similar system, making use of an office or a clearinghouse connected to the court. You are entitled to a copy of your payment record from any of these programs and can get it by a verbal or written request.

It's a good idea to call before dropping in so you can check with the program for its exact procedures to get a record. If, however, the staff delays more than a week or two, you may want to drop in and be insistent. It should take only a minute to make you a copy, and there's no reason you should have to wait weeks while your request sits in a dusty corner.

If you're receiving payments privately, you'll have to make your own payment record. A lawyer or child support worker can help you, but you can save time and money by doing it yourself. We'll look first at how to record present and future payments, then at how to gather and reconstruct a past payment record.

Whenever possible, encourage the noncustodial parent to make his payments by check or money order. If you do this as a habit—and particularly if he'll agree in writing to pay by check only—it will discourage any later false claims of cash payments. If the noncustodial parent says in court that he's been making cash payments, you'll be able to say to the judge, "Your Honor, I'm afraid he doesn't pay by cash. As this written statement shows, he agreed last March to pay by check, and there have been no cash payments since." Then the burden will be on the noncustodial parent to produce canceled checks to prove payment.

The other advantage to payment by check is that you can document your own records with copies of all checks you receive. This will help guard against the use of falsified records by the noncustodial parent. If, for example, he claims he paid you $200 on August 1, but your copy of his check for that date shows it was only for $100, you'll have no trouble proving your claim. For this reason, you should be sure to photocopy all checks and money orders you receive before cashing them.

Of course, this approach isn't right for everyone since some people just don't use checks as a habit. You might quite reasonably fear that insisting on payment by check could decrease or stop payment altogether. If the noncustodial parent has $100 cash in hand ready to give you, it may not seem like such a good idea to insist he go to a bank, have a money order made and come back another day.

A good substitute approach is to go now to any drugstore or

stationery store and purchase (for a dollar or so) a cash receipt book. It should have two parts to every receipt: the actual receipt for you to fill in with the date and amount of payment and give to the noncustodial parent, and the receipt stub to fill in with the same information and keep for your records.

In addition to saving receipt stubs or copies of checks and money orders, you should keep a careful record of all payments due, all payments actually made and the difference or deficit. There's a Child Support Payment Record form in the appendix of this book that you can use to keep your record. An example of how to record entries for a sample month follows.

Let's say, for example, that in the month of January, 1986, you were due to receive $300 child support, $150 of it on the first and the other $150 on the fifteenth. Instead, you received $75 on the twelfth, $50 on the twenty-second, and a bag of groceries on the twenty-fifth. Here's how your Child Support Payment Record would look that month:

CHILD SUPPORT PAYMENT RECORD
YEAR   1986

MONTH	Payment Due Date	Amount	Actual Payments Date	Amount	Deficit
JANUARY	01-01-86	$150⁰⁰	01-12-86	$75⁰⁰	
FEBRUARY	01-15-86	$150⁰⁰	01-22-86	$50⁰⁰	
MARCH					
APRIL					
MAY					
JUNE					
JULY					
AUGUST					
SEPTEMBER					
OCTOBER					
NOVEMBER					
DECEMBER					
MONTHLY TOTAL		$300⁰⁰		$125⁰⁰	$175⁰⁰

As you can see, you start by writing down the dates and amounts of payments due and the dates and amounts of actual payments made. At the end of the month, you total each and subtract to find the deficit. This gives you a clear monthly total of all you've received and all you are owed.

Note that no entry is made for the groceries. That's because purchases not ordered by the court or requested by you aren't considered payment under the support order. They're considered a gift and will not reduce the monthly support obligation.

These records will be extremely helpful in the future if you need to collect overdue support. They will document for the judge, as well as for your lawyer or child support worker, exactly what you are owed.

If you are working now to collect past unpaid support, you should try to make a payment record for those past months, too. If you have old records of payments made, you can transfer those old records onto the Child Support Payment Record form to compute exactly how much is still owed. Don't throw out your original records, though. They're your best proof that your payment figures are accurate.

With all you've had to think about while raising the children on your own, it's quite possible you haven't in the past kept a formal payment record. In that case, you'll have to reconstruct one as best you can from memory and what records you can gather.

If it's your standard habit to deposit support payments into your checking account, for example, perhaps you can go through old checkbooks and bank records to track down past payments that way. If you received any alimony and reported it on your income taxes, you can get yearly totals from your old tax returns. (If you no longer have them handy, you can get them by completing and mailing the IRS form 4506, "Request for Copy of a Tax Return.")

As you make your record, give the noncustodial parent the benefit of the doubt anytime you're not sure whether payments were made. There's a very important reason for this. If you go into court saying, for example, that no payments were made during the first half of 1984, and the noncustodial parent produces two canceled checks from that time period, it may make all your records look unreliable. Quite possibly the judge will be hesitant to enforce past unpaid support at all.

For the same reason, you should discuss openly with your lawyer or child support worker what you do and do not remember. For example, suppose you know that the noncustodial parent paid no more than $200 to $300 in 1983, but you don't remember exactly when or in what amounts per payment. Say just that, give him credit for the $300 to be safe and don't try to fill out the Child Support Payment Record. Your lawyer will argue your case on the strength of your testimony, the testimony of any witnesses you may have and the fact that the noncustodial parent has no records that prove that payment of over $300 was made.

Documenting unpaid support yourself is always a somewhat riskier method than having it recorded through an agency or clearinghouse. No matter how carefully you keep your records, some judges may view them as less reliable than the records of a neutral third party.

If you do find yourself facing credibility battles in court over your payment records versus the noncustodial parent's, you may want to think about using an agency or a clearinghouse, or even just having payments made through your lawyer. You may experience a slight delay in receiving payments as they're processed, but the increased credibility may be worth it.

17

Collection Methods

There are several methods available for collecting child support, whether as a lump sum repayment of unpaid past support or on a continuing basis. Most are available both through your local OCSE office or through the traditional legal system.

DEMAND FOR PAYMENT

The first step in collecting child support is usually a formal demand for payment. Of course, you've probably been demanding payment for months or even years, but a formal demand is a little different. Basically it's a way of letting the noncustodial parent know you will use legal collection remedies if support isn't paid promptly. It's an inexpensive, easy way to get the nonsupporter's attention; to say, in effect, "You might as well pay now, because it will save you the headache of going to court and then having to pay."

If you think it might get results, you can make the first formal demand for payment yourself, even before you go to an agency or a lawyer. Simply write a brief typed letter requesting immediate payment of support due and explaining that you will seek legal remedies if support is not paid. *Don't* offer any deals (such as that you'll overlook past-due support if continuing support is paid). To emphasize the seriousness of the letter, you could, for two or three dollars, send it by registered mail.

Of course, once you say you'll take a certain action in a demand for payment, it's important that you do it. If you say in the letter, "If I don't receive payment by February 1, I will seek legal remedies," you need to be ready to open your case with a lawyer or an agency during the first week of February. Then, when the noncustodial parent gets a demand letter from the lawyer or agency during the second week of February, he'll know you mean business.

Agencies or lawyers will follow a similar method. Sometimes, again to increase the impact, they use mailgrams. Often their demands will notify the nonsupporter to appear for an interview on a certain day to discuss payment. If he does, and suitable arrangements can be made, a court action can be avoided.

CONTEMPT OF COURT

All traditional courts have the power to enforce their orders. If a person willfully disobeys a court order, the judge can find him in *contempt of court* and impose a fine or send him to jail. Generally a person who is jailed for contempt of court can get out of jail anytime he arranges to obey the court order (for example, by paying ordered support).

Jailing for contempt of court is generally used only as a last resort in child support cases, but the knowledge that it's available can affect the case from the beginning. Some nonsupporters can and will try every trick in the book to avoid paying support, but many will prefer paying to risking a stay in jail. Particularly if a judge is known to use contempt jailing powers when needed, most noncustodial parents will pay reliably.

Contempt of court is always officially available through the traditional legal system (although as a practical matter, not all judges are willing to use it to enforce payment of support). Whether it will continue to be available for those pursuing cases through their local OCSE is less clear. Under the federal Child Support Enforcement Amendments of 1984, requiring states to develop streamlined procedures for child support cases, there is no specific requirement that contempt of court powers be available. This could create enforcement problems, since jailing for contempt, however unpleasant, has always been a key way courts of all kinds make sure their orders are followed.

You can find out if contempt powers are available in OCSE cases in your area by checking with your local OCSE office. If they're not, you may want to raise this as a problem for action by a local custodial parents' group.

INCOME WITHHOLDING

If the noncustodial parent receives any form of regular income, whether it's wages, pension or government benefits, there's a good chance you can have child support regularly deducted from that income. The child support will then automatically be sent to you, either directly or through an agency such as the OCSE.

The most common form of income withholding is a wage assignment. Under the new federal child support law, all state OCSE offices must make use of wage assignment techniques. Exact procedures vary by state, but the basic principal is quite simple.

When a child support order is first entered, employer information is included. If the noncustodial parent at any later time becomes one month or more behind in payments, the OCSE will notify the employer to begin deducting the monthly child support payments from wages and sending them to you or the OCSE office. No new hearing will be necessary to begin operation of the wage assignment, and the only acceptable grounds for the noncustodial parent to contest it will be a mistake of fact (e.g., that he did pay and the OCSE records were mistaken).

Under the law, employers must cooperate and may not fire or demote the noncustodial parent because of the wage assignment. Actually most employers agree without concern or complaint. Even noncustodial parents seem to get used to wage assignments with time, and some prefer to set up a voluntary wage assignment right from the beginning. It's easier for them not having to write and send a check each month, and they're less tempted to spend money they never see.

There is a limit to how much of a paycheck can be deducted by a wage assignment. If the noncustodial parent is not supporting anyone besides you and/or your children, up to 60 percent of his after-taxes paycheck can go to the wage assignment. If he does have other dependents, such as a new spouse or other children, only 50 percent of the paycheck will be assignable. (Of course, given the generally low levels of child support, these limits usually aren't reached anyway. Also, the two figures can be increased to 65 and 55 percent respectively if part of the wage assignment is to pay past overdue support.)

The federal legislation doesn't specifically require that this simplified wage assignment method be available to non-OCSE cases. If you're considering using a private lawyer instead of the OCSE, be sure to ask about the availability of wage assignments and whether procedures through the traditional legal system will be as efficient as the OCSE procedures.

Effective procedures are available for withholding the wages of a federal employee. The OCSE is a good source for information and assistance, as are some private lawyers.

Some states also allow withholding of child support from other types of income, such as pensions, private trusts or annuities, worker's compensation, disability benefits or other government benefits. The procedures used are similar to wage assignment procedures. Check with a lawyer or the local OCSE.

MILITARY DEPENDENT ALLOTMENTS

A similar method is available if the noncustodial parent is in the armed forces. All members of the military are entitled to a pay allotment for any dependent child, with the amount based on the member's pay and grade. The allotment is allowed only if the service member is actively supporting the child and is in addition to the member's regular pay. Dependent allotments are available with both active military pay and military retirement pay. In general, they can be higher than most court orders for child support (by a parent at a similar income level).

You can arrange to have your child's dependent allotment sent to you by the military, either directly or through the local OCSE. Once the arrangement is made, it will continue without interruption even if the noncustodial parent is transferred to another military base or to active duty overseas.

The simplest way to make this arrangement is if the noncustodial parent will agree in writing to have the allotment check sent to you. Since it won't decrease his paycheck, and he's not entitled to receive the allotment himself if he doesn't support, he should agree.

If he doesn't, it's a good idea to contact his commanding officer by registered letter or phone to explain the problem and request assistance. Every branch of the service has regulations stating that it is the legal and moral obligation of service members to support their children and that commanding officers have a duty to advise service members of their obligation to do so. In some branches of the service, refusal to support one's children can even result in a disciplinary action or lack of promotion.

(This commendable policy is unfortunately limited to encouraging support of children born to mothers who are U.S. citizens. The U.S. military has been severely criticized for their noncooperation in support enforcement, or even in revealing the father's location, in the many cases in which children are fathered and abandoned by U.S. servicemen overseas.)

If, after contacting the commanding officer, you are still unable to get a voluntary assignment, you can seek an assignment through the family court or OCSE system. Basically these systems use the regular wage assignment procedure just described, with the service branch as the employer required to deduct and send child support. Although in theory you could seek a child support amount higher or lower than the allotment amount, the usual practice is to use the allotment amount as evidence of ability to pay and seek that amount as the child support award.

TAX REFUNDS

One way to collect owed back support is by *intercepting* (collecting before he does) the noncustodial parent's tax refund. This method is available in every state through the OCSE and can be used to intercept both state and federal tax refunds.

Unfortunately there are a couple of problems with this method. Obviously it's available only once a year and only if you act before the refund is sent. Also, before the OCSE will help you intercept the federal refund, $500 in back support must be owed. (The state OCSE can further limit interceptions by requiring that the $500 must be support owed since *they* began trying to collect for you. Whether state OCSE offices will impose that further limit is not yet known.) Finally, the Internal Revenue Service must notify the noncustodial parent before sending you the amount withheld, giving him—and any new spouse with whom he filed jointly—an opportunity to object. If they do, their objections will be reviewed before sending you the money, and any amount belonging to the jointly filing spouse will go to her instead.

Clearly this method has a lot of limitations. Still, it might be worth considering if a large amount of support is owed and the noncustodial parent has a high income, making a large refund likely. Also, since states may be less restrictive about intercepting state tax refunds, you could ask about that.

SEIZING PROPERTY AND ASSETS

In Tallahassee, Florida, there's a judge who regularly asks non-supporting parents how they got to court that day. If the answer is that they drove, the judge is quite likely to have the car seized on the spot. Other judges, impatient with nonsupporters wearing gold watches and other jewelry, will collect the jewelry before the hearing ends.

The legal process of seizing property, known as *attachment,* can be a very effective means of support collection. All kinds of property—boats, motorcycles, even houses—can be attached. Then the nonsupporter is given a choice: pay the support you owe or we'll sell your property to pay the debt.

There's also a similar process for taking possession of bank accounts and other financial assets. In most states this is called *garnishment.* The assets garnished would, of course, go directly to pay support owed.

To get either an attachment or a garnishment, you first need to have a final judgment showing the exact amount of support owed. You can get this, after a hearing in which you show that payments are overdue, from the court that originally made the support order.

In some states (as in the examples just given), the same court that finds that payments are overdue can order an attachment or a garnishment immediately if you have information about the property to be seized. In other states, you'll need to take the judgment from the first court and go to a different court to get the attachment or garnishment.

Both private attorneys and local OCSE offices may use attachment or garnishment as tools to collect support. However, since these are methods most often used to collect from wealthier nonsupporters—and since many OCSE offices are used to handling lower-income cases—you may find that private lawyers will be more experienced with them.

REPORTING TO CREDIT AGENCIES

Technically, reporting to credit agencies is not a way to collect support. It is, however, a good way to make it less comfortable for a noncustodial parent to *not* pay support. If a credit agency knows that a parent owes a child support debt, he may be denied credit, making it difficult to buy a house, car or other desired property. The parent may then be motivated to pay the debt owed and restore his credit.

State OCSE offices are required under the new federal law to report to credit agencies all parents who owe more than $1000 in back support. However, they *may* report much smaller amounts owed. If you think it might be helpful in your case, you should request that a report be made.

You or a private lawyer can also make a report to a credit

agency, but only if there is an actual court judgment showing the exact amount owed. This is to avoid any inaccurate or one-sided reports.

Quite possibly you'll find it will be necessary to use more than one enforcement tool to collect your support. For example, you might use an attachment to collect back support, then follow up with a wage assignment for collecting continuing support.

It's a good idea to act as promptly as possible in collecting overdue support. If you let a few payments slide without making enforcement efforts, the noncustodial parent may conclude that he can pay or not pay according to his own convenience. Worse, once a poor payment pattern begins, it's hard to break the habit. The noncustodial parent may begin spending the support money on his own expenses, leaving little or nothing to collect when you do begin enforcement efforts.

If, on the other hand, you work from the beginning to enforce a good payment record, you're more likely to continue receiving support without the need for future enforcement actions. In the long run, it will mean fewer trips to the courthouse and more support for your children.

18

Anticipating Defenses

There are really only three types of defenses most commonly made in a child support case. They are:

- "I've really been paying all along."
- "I haven't paid because I can't afford that much."
- "I haven't paid, but she's not acting right either, Judge."

You've already learned, in Chapters 10, 11 and 16, how to disprove the first two defenses. This chapter will focus on the third.

In a sense, the "she's not acting right" defense is not a true defense at all. It's an attempt to open other issues and, if possible, redirect the attention of the court away from the nonsupport issue. It may be a claim that you aren't spending child support money on the children or aren't raising them properly; or that you're interfering with visitation or turning the children against their other parent. The claim itself may not have much truth *in fact*, but it may well *feel* true to the noncustodial parent.

Unfortunately the old saying that the best defense is a good offense sometimes works in child support cases. However you feel about any of these claims, it's important that you be prepared to respond to them seriously, because many judges take them very seriously indeed. You want to avoid the problem by resolving differences early if possible and to prepare to defend yourself against false accusations if you can't resolve problems by agreement.

The first step in dealing with these claims is trying to understand the motivation behind them. In most cases, the desire to avoid paying child support is as much an emotional issue as an economic one. Hard as it is to see sometimes, the anger and hurt that many noncustodial parents feel over a family breakup is real and understandable—even if their response is totally misdirected. This is not to say that you've done anything wrong but only that a family breakup is painful and confusing for everyone concerned.

At the risk of reinforcing old stereotypes, it's helpful, to really understand the problem, to look at common male and female patterns of relating. Most women in our society were raised to expect that they should be the emotional caretakers in their families—of the children, of course, but also to some degree of their husbands. In return, they could expect financial support from the man. Even in families in which both parents worked outside the home, this pattern usually continued to some degree, if only because wage discrimination kept women earning far less than men. Small wonder, then, that women—many of whom never asked for this particular "bargain" but who kept their part nonetheless—feel betrayed when they find themselves continuing to raise the children but without the father's support.

Yet many men feel disillusioned, too. The same social roles that automatically gave the woman the caretaking job also deprived the men of much chance at family involvement. Even if they accepted, encouraged or insisted upon those sex role divisions in their own families, they may still on some level feel hurt and deprived by them.

That's not to say that *you* have ever deprived your children's father of involvement with them. Quite possibly you've encouraged it, only to hear him say he's too busy with work or even that he can't be bothered. But if he's been raised to believe he has no skills with children or that child care is unmanly, those excuses may just have been a way of hiding his own fears and socially ingrained lack of confidence.

So where does child support fit in? Isn't that just what men were raised to feel they could do successfully—provide financial support? Well, yes, but as part of a package. It's as if society (through the teachings of parents, schools, movies, books and television) dictated a role for men but also made them a promise. "Be tough and responsible, support your family and don't show your real feelings. In return, you'll be the 'head of the household,' a man of power and respect."

Today many men, like many women, find themselves dissatisfied with the old roles. As long as things seem to be working —as long as the family is together and the man gets the attention and authority he's been raised to expect—he might well not rock the boat, even if it feels awful at times not being very involved emotionally with the children. Deep down, he might suspect that so-called power in the family is a poor substitute for real emotional involvement, but at least it feels safe, in that it's a role he's been taught to play since childhood.

But if the family breaks up, the man may find himself feeling increasingly lonely and alienated. Not too confident about his emotional skills, he may blame his insecurity on the children's mother: "You've turned the kids against me." "You won't let me visit them." He may seek to regain a sense of power and control in the family: "You don't discipline the kids properly. The judge should make you do it my way." Finally, he may withhold child support as a way of lashing out in hurt and anger. Again, to avoid responsibility for his actions, he may project the blame: "Oh, you'd just spend it on yourself anyway." He focuses his anger on the woman and children, because it's too confusing to be angry at something vague like society or a set of unfair promises or his frustration that he never learned to be comfortable with his children.

To say that all that is understandable, of course, is not to say that it's acceptable behavior. Children still have to eat, however their parents feel. They also need the security of a home life free of angry power plays that put them in the middle. You can have some understanding and empathy for this kind of negative behavior but still work to protect yourself and your children from its effects.

RESISTING POWER PLAYS

In fact, understanding can help you avoid getting entangled in power struggles, including ones that could later come back to haunt you in court. For example, suppose your children's father consistently creates visitation problems by showing up hours late, on the wrong day, intoxicated or with plans for the day that are inappropriate for children. You could easily assume he was not interested in visiting the children and was only trying to create trouble. It would be quite understandable if you told him that and then refused to allow the children to see him at all.

Yet that kind of behavior, wrong as it is, might well reflect the noncustodial parent's fear that he couldn't relate to the children well even if he tried. By setting up a situation in which he knows you'll refuse to let the children see him, he can blame his alienation from the children on you. "I tried to visit them, but she wouldn't let me." He can also tell this to the judge later, in defending himself against child support nonpayment claims (or even protesting the custody arrangements).

Of course, you can't responsibly send the children off for a visit with their father at nine on a school night or when he's been drinking or is on the way to a poker game. But you can say to him, in an honest and respectful manner, "The kids really love you and want to see you. You're important to them, and I think that's great. But we all feel disappointed and unhappy when we expect you and things don't work out. I'd really like to see you having an active part in their life, but that's only possible when we all know we can depend on you."

If possible, plan a conversation like this in advance, at a neutral time and place, with the children not there. You might, for example, make a plan to meet for lunch in a public place. Be sure to try to listen to the noncustodial parent's feelings, even if he doesn't always state them directly. If he seems angry, for example, ask him if he is, and why. If he can answer you honestly, it may be the beginning of some communication and understanding between you.

All that's hard to do, of course, especially if tempers are already high. You may want to consider a few mutual counseling sessions if the problem is persistent and you both want to see it resolved.

PROTECTING YOURSELF IN COURT

In the meantime, you need to plan ahead to protect yourself and your children against the "she's not acting right" defenses should they ever come up in court. There are several ways you can do this.

The same diary you learned about keeping in Chapter 13 will also serve you in this situation. At the end of each day, jot down a few brief notes about whatever you did with or for the children. Also record any interactions with the noncustodial parent. This will serve as your record in the future if it's claimed that you're not caring for the children well or are turning them against the noncustodial parent. It won't be absolute proof, of course, but it will help bolster your testimony about what has happened in the past.

If you have any conversations with the noncustodial parent about visitation problems, you might want to follow up with a short, polite letter emphasizing that you favor continuing visitation as long as the guidelines for the children's safety and security are followed. Keep a photocopy of the letter with your diary as proof against the claim that you've been resisting visitation.

You should also make it a point to see that there *is* no truth to the charge that you're resisting visitation, except to protect the children's safety and security. Specifically you should know that nonpayment of child support is not considered by family courts to be good cause for you to resist visitation. Although it may seem to you that a nonsupporting parent doesn't have the right to see the children, the court probably won't see it that way. It's often hard to tell which came first, the nonsupport or the withholding of visitation. Since most judges are male, they may even be inclined to take the man's side. A few have even taken the drastic step of "solving" a nonsupport, nonvisitation case by switching custody to the father without any proof that the switch would be in the children's best interests.

For this reason if for no other, you should be very sure to refuse visitation *only* if the children's immediate safety or security is at stake. If the problems can be solved by other means —whether a frank talk or a legal action—it's best to follow those other means. In any case, due to the risks, you should be in touch with your lawyer anytime there are serious visitation problems.

A claim that you aren't spending child support money on the children is probably the easiest to disprove. Child support amounts, even when they're paid, tend to be lower than the children's needs. All you need to do to safeguard against this claim is to keep records of how you spend your family income each month. Some expenses, such as clothing, schoolbooks, lessons and toys, will clearly be money spent on the children. Others, such as food, rent and utilities, can be credited as partly spent on the children. For example, if you live alone with two children, you can credit two-thirds of the food and rent costs as money spent on the children.

In general, your response to the general problem of power-play defenses will be a combination of sensitive diplomacy and effective action. As best as you can, you'll try to avoid the problem by dealing honestly and fairly with the noncustodial parent in an atmosphere of firmness and respect. If he persists in trying to justify nonsupport through angry accusations, however, you'll be prepared to defend yourself against those accusations. Most important, you'll then be in a good position to redirect the court's attention to the more pressing problem of nonsupport.

19

Creative Collection

In Orange County, Florida, a feisty group of custodial parents doesn't stop at fighting nonsupporters—they take on the court system, too. Though it is humorously named, the Children Against Deadbeat Dads takes its job seriously. When local judges failed to respond to citizen pleas for tougher child support enforcement, CADD was out in force to picket the courthouse.

"Picketing is only one way we make our views known," says Marj Van Brackle, an active member. "We also lobby and hold public information meetings. But I have to say that the picketing helped bring instant media attention to a very real problem."

The Women's Network in Montgomery County, Pennsylvania, found picketing effective in another way. Frustrated by attempts to collect from wealthy self-employed nonsupporters, they decided to embarrass the men into paying. With signs reading THE OWNER OF THIS COMPANY DOES NOT SUPPORT HIS CHILDREN, group members paraded in front of the nonsupporters' businesses. In short order, the men paid.

The Association for Children for Enforcement of Support (ACES) of Toledo, Ohio, focuses more on citizen education. With a mixed female and male membership of over a thousand, ACES tries to see all sides of divorce conflicts. "Child support is the worst problem," says member Pam Cady matter-of-factly. "We see wrong on both sides between custodial and noncustodial parents, and I can understand the feelings of each. But there are just too many children going without because child support isn't being paid."

To address the emotional toll of divorce, ACES offers peer support groups for children and informal peer counseling for their parents. To tackle the more practical problem of child support enforcement, they provide "legal rights and remedies" seminars on collecting through the court system.

It's a strong and growing network. All across the country, custodial parents are organizing to coax, prod and, if necessary, pressure a sometimes slumbering bureaucracy into action. Parents Enforcing Court Ordered Support (PECOS) of Connecticut conducts a formal court-watch program to identify and publicize the actions of judges who don't take support enforcement seriously. Virginians Organized in the Interest of Children's Entitlement to Support (VOICES) holds training sessions with practice trials to help prepare custodial parents to represent themselves in court. A Texas group, Parents for Kids, discovered that a local district attorney was charging unauthorized fees to custodial parents who were seeking support enforcement. By taking their findings to state-elected officials, the group eventually managed to have the policy changed and the district attorney replaced.

Child support is everyone's battle, because no child is safe until all our children are safe. By working for better enforcement, we can help bring our children the security—and the support—they need and deserve.

Whether you work with a parents' group or pursue your children's support case independently, you'll be making a social contribution that can't be measured in dollars. For your children, the benefits will be a better life with more opportunities. You'll also be showing them that family is important—and so are they.

One mother of two small boys who struggled for two years before she began collecting child support regularly described her feelings this way: "There were times I almost threw in the towel. Sometimes I kept going on anger, sometimes idealism. We really needed the money, and I couldn't ignore that. Mostly, though, I just wanted my kids to know I thought they deserved to be supported by both parents, and that I was willing to do what it took to see that they were. For that alone, I'm glad I stuck it out."

If you've never been involved in a legal action before, you'll probably be surprised at how well you do. Most people feel nervous the first time they go before a judge, take part in an administrative hearing or have to make a crucial decision—but they end up doing just fine. Certainly the challenges are no greater than (and may well be less than) the everyday challenges of raising a child alone.

As you pursue your case, your efforts will help pave a road for others behind you. With every successful enforcement action, the system becomes a little stronger. Just as the efforts of others before you brought us new laws and enforcement programs, your efforts will help build greater efficiency in those new programs.

You'll be part of a continuing chain of parents who care enough to struggle for the welfare of our children. Because of you and others like you, our children can hope for a better, more secure life.

Appendix

CASE INFORMATION FORM

INFORMATION ABOUT YOU

Name _____
       Last   First   Middle   Maiden

Address _____
_____

Date of Birth _____ Social Security Number _____
Phone (home) _____ (work) _____
Are you employed? _____ What do you earn? _____
   Employer name _____ Employer phone _____
   Employer address _____
   Your position _____ How long employed? _____
Do you receive AFDC? _____ How much? _____
   For which child(ren)? _____
Do you have any other source of income? If so, describe:
   Source _____ Amount _____
_____

Are you now married? _____ Spouse's name _____
   When married? _____ Do you live with spouse now? ____
   Is spouse employed? _____ Position _____
Were you formerly married? If so, list former spouse(s), date of
each marriage, date of each divorce.
_____
_____
_____

** BRING COPIES OF ANY MARRIAGE CERTIFICATES,
DIVORCE DECREES, OR SUPPORT ORDERS.

What are your goals in this legal action? (Check all that apply.)

Find missing noncustodial parent _____

Establish paternity _____

Get a child support order and collect support _____

Collect overdue child support from existing order _____

Get a divorce _____

Divide marital property _____

Get an order for alimony and collect it _____

Collect overdue alimony from existing order _____

Please list all members of your household:

Name	Age	Relationship to you

INFORMATION ABOUT THE CHILD(REN)
FOR WHOM SUPPORT IS SOUGHT

Note: Fill out separately for each child for whom you're seeking support.

*** Child's name_____ Date of birth_____
Place of birth_____ Sex_____ Social Security No._____
Lives with you?_____ Ever lived with anyone else?_____
School_____ Grade_____
Were you married to noncustodial parent when child was
conceived or born?_____
If not, has paternity ever been established? When and how?_____

_____

If not, does father agree he is the father?_____
Does child know and visit noncustodial parent?_____
Does child have any special medical or educational needs?_____

_____

*** Child's name_____ Date of birth_____
Place of birth_____ Sex_____ Social Security No._____
Lives with you?_____ Ever lived with anyone else?_____
School_____ Grade_____
Were you married to noncustodial parent when child was
conceived or born?_____
If not, has paternity ever been established? When and how?_____

_____

If not, does father agree he is the father?_____
Does child know and visit noncustodial parent?_____
Does child have any special medical or educational needs?_____

_____

*** Child's name_____ Date of birth_____
   Place of birth_____ Sex_____ Social Security No._____
   Lives with you?_____ Ever lived with anyone else?_____
   School_____ Grade_____
Were you married to noncustodial parent when child was
conceived or born?_____
If not, has paternity ever been established? When and how?_____

_____

If not, does father agree he is the father?_____
Does child know and visit noncustodial parent?_____
Does child have any special medical or educational needs?_____

_____

*** Child's name_____ Date of birth_____
   Place of birth_____ Sex_____ Social Security No._____
   Lives with you?_____ Ever lived with anyone else?_____
   School_____ Grade_____
Were you married to noncustodial parent when child was
conceived or born?_____
If not, has paternity ever been established? When and how?_____

_____

If not, does father agree he is the father?_____
Does child know and visit noncustodial parent?_____
Does child have any special medical or educational needs?_____

_____

INFORMATION ABOUT THE
NONCUSTODIAL PARENT

Note: Leave blank anything you don't know.

Name_____

      Last   First   Middle

Address_____

_____

Date of Birth_____ Social Security Number_____

Phone (home)_____ (work)_____

If you don't know current address, do you know a former address?

_____

_____

Is he employed?_____ What does he earn?_____

    Employer name_____ Employer phone_____

    Employer address_____

His position_____ How long employed?_____

If you don't know current employment, do you know of past employment?

    Employer name_____ Employer phone_____

    Employer address_____

His position_____ How long employed?_____

    Is he now married?_____ Spouse's name_____

    Living with spouse?_____ Any children in the home?_____

    Is spouse employed?_____ Her position?_____

Does he have other children? Who; where are they; does he support them?

_____

_____

_____

Has he previously been married? If so, when; to whom; when divorced; does he pay alimony?_____

_____

_____

Does he own any of the following?

	Description	Location	Approx. Value
Car or truck			
Car or truck			
Checking account			
Savings account			
House			
Other real estate			
Stocks, bonds, etc.			
Pension			
Other			

Do you know of any way he might get money or property in the future (such as inheritance, debts owed, lawsuit pending, etc.)?

_____

_____

Does he have credit or the ability to borrow? _____

_____

Was he ever ordered to pay you child support? _____ When? _____
How much? _____ How often? _____
Was he ever ordered to pay you alimony? _____ When? _____
How much? _____ How often? _____
Is any support now being paid? _____
How much and how often? _____

_____

Date last payment received? _____
Usual method of payment (check, cash, etc.)? _____
To whom are payments made? _____
Have you attempted to enforce support before? _____ Describe:

_____

_____

_____

_____

_____

_____

BUDGET CHECKLIST

Shelter
___ Rent or mortgage payment
___ Property and local taxes
___ Home isurance
___ Utilities (gas, electric, fuel, water, phone)
___ Repairs and upkeep
___ Snow and garbage removal, lawn care, weatherizing
___ Other

Household
___ Household employees
___ Furniture purchases and repairs
___ Appliance purchases and repairs
___ Blankets, sheets, towels, etc.
___ Cleaning supplies
___ Paper products
___ Rug and furniture cleaning
___ Other

Food
___ Groceries
___ Workday lunches
___ Children's lunches

Health care
___ Insurance
___ Medical visits
___ Dentist and orthodontist
___ Medicine (prescription and over-the-counter)
___ Counseling and therapy
___ Glasses, hearing aids, etc.
___ Other

Transportation
___ Public (buses, trains, taxis)
___ Car payments, insurance and license costs
___ Car repairs, gas and oil
___ Parking and tolls

Clothing
— Adult clothing purchases
— Children's clothing purchases
— Dry cleaning, laundry, mending and alterations

Education and child care
— Day care
— After-school care
— Baby-sitting
— School tuition
— Books and supplies
— Extracurricular activities (sports, field trips, etc.)
— Lessons (music, dance, art, etc.)
— Magazines, books, records
— Educational toys and learning aids
— Children's summer camp

Financial security
— Savings
— Life insurance
— IRA or other pension fund
— Other

Recreation
— Home (parties, liquor, cigarettes, other)
— Meals out
— Movies, theater, concerts, etc.
— Sporting events
— Toys, television, stereo
— Clubs, hobbies, sports equipment
— Vacations

Personal
— Physical fitness
— Haircuts and personal care
— Soap, shampoo, toilet articles
— Other

Loan and bill payments
— Charge accounts
— Installment purchases
— Education loans

__ Personal loans
__ Other

Dues, gifts and contributions
__ Union or organization dues
__ Workplace social obligations
__ Birthdays, anniversaries, etc.
__ Christmas and other holidays
__ Charitable contributions

Income taxes
__ City
__ State
__ Federal
__ Social Security

Other Family Expenses

CHILD SUPPORT PAYMENT RECORD
YEAR _____

MONTH	Payment Due		Actual Payments		Deficit
	Date	Amount	Date	Amount	
JANUARY					
MONTHLY TOTAL					
FEBRUARY					
MONTHLY TOTAL					
MARCH					
MONTHLY TOTAL					
APRIL					
MONTHLY TOTAL					

CHILD SUPPORT PAYMENT RECORD
YEAR _____

MONTH	Payment Due		Actual Payments		Deficit
	Date	Amount	Date	Amount	
MAY					
MONTHLY TOTAL					
JUNE					
MONTHLY TOTAL					
JULY					
MONTHLY TOTAL					
AUGUST					
MONTHLY TOTAL					

CHILD SUPPORT PAYMENT RECORD
YEAR _____

MONTH	Payment Due		Actual Payments		Deficit
	Date	Amount	Date	Amount	
SEPTEMBER					
MONTHLY TOTAL					
OCTOBER					
MONTHLY TOTAL					
NOVEMBER					
MONTHLY TOTAL					
DECEMBER					
MONTHLY TOTAL					

Notes

Preface

1. Of the 8.4 million women raising children alone in 1981, only 2.9 million received any support at all from the children's father. Bureau of the Census, U.S. Department of Commerce, *Child Support and Alimony: 1981* (Advance Report), Series P-23, No. 124.
2. In 1978, 31 percent of all female-headed families were below the poverty level, defined as $6662 a year for a nonfarm family of four. Bureau of the Census, U.S. Department of Commerce, *Characteristics of the Population Below the Poverty Level: 1978*, Series P-60, No. 124.
3. Weitzman, "The Economics of Divorce: Social and Economic Consequences of Property, Alimony, and Child Support Awards, *UCLA Law Review* 28:1181, 1245 (1981).
4. Summary of Government Accounting Office Report, 120 Cong. Rec. 38196-98 (Dec. 4, 1974).
5. The Child Support Enforcement Amendments of 1984 (amending the Social Security Act).
6. Most fathers neither request custody nor, when custody is then awarded to the mother, pay child support.

   Even in California, widely believed to be a trendsetter state in terms of changing sex roles, fathers request custody in less than one out of ten cases. Weitzman and Dixon, "Child Custody Awards: Legal Standards and Empirical Patterns for Child Custody, Support and Visitation After Divorce," *UCD Law Review* 12:471, 502–02 (1979).

   For statistics on nonsupport, see Note 1.
7. U.S. Department of Labor, Women's Bureau, *The Employment of Women, General Diagnosis of Developments and Issues*, April 1980.
8. A 1979 Harvard-based project found women still doing all or most of the household chores: 90 percent of the women and 85 percent of the men interviewed said the wife was the one who changed the diapers. And, in 1980, surveys by advertising agencies found men still resistant to housework and wanting most in a wife "a good mother who would

assume responsibility for the children." *New York Times,* April 3, 1979 and Nov. 1, 1980. See also Robinson, John P., *How Americans Use Time: A Social-Psychological Analysis* (New York: Holt, Rinehart & Winston, Praeger Books, 1977).

1. Taking Charge of Your Case

1. Aspaklaria, Shelley, and Gerson Geltner, *Everything You Want to Know About Your Husband's Money . . . And Need to Know Before the Divorce* (New York: Thomas Y. Crowell, 1980), p. 190.

2. The Office of Child Support Enforcement

1. These and numerous other myths are exploded in B. Leyser and A. Blong, *Beyond the Myths—Families Helped by the AFDC Program,* available from the Center on Social Welfare Policy and Law, 95 Madison Avenue, New York, NY 10016 ($1.75 each).

3. Collecting Across State Lines

1. As of January, 1985, only three states regularly charge fees to custodial parents pursuing a URESA case: Alaska ($25 filing fee), Iowa (rules being developed to charge in cases where family is not receiving AFDC) and Oklahoma (10% of each support check is withheld if family is not receiving AFDC). All other states either charge no fees or will waive fees if the family cannot afford to pay.
2. See URESA Administrative Procedures Handbook, National Reciprocal and Family Support Enforcement Association, October 1981, p. 35.
3. See, e.g., state listings for Indiana, Iowa, Kentucky and Mississippi in the Referral Guide described in note 5.
4. URESA Statute Matrix, National Conference of State Legislatures, 1983. Included in the Referral Guide described in note 5.
5. This guide, the National Roster and URESA/IV-D Referral Guide, is available for $10.50 plus $1.00 handling from:
National Reciprocal and Family Support Enforcement Association
P.O. Box 6068
Des Moines, Iowa 50309
(515) 262-6807
While the guide may be useful to custodial parents' groups, it's probably not worth the investment for just one case, since you can get the information on your case from your local URESA office.

4. Tough Remedies for Tough Cases

1. The classic study of the effects of jailing upon child-support enforcement is David Chambers, *Making Fathers Pay: The Enforcement of*

Child Support (University of Chicago Press, 1979). This massive study of twenty-eight Michigan counties (containing nearly 85% of the state's residents) is actually a study of a civil enforcement system that depends heavily upon the power of civil courts to impose jailing for contempt of court. This system, known as the Friend of the Court system, is really quite unique to Michigan. Except for the lack of due process protections for the nonsupporting parents, however, the system operates much as criminal nonsupport programs in other states do. For this reason, and because *Making Fathers Pay* is the only comprehensive study of its kind, reference will be made to Chambers's findings in these notes.

2. See Chambers, pp. 231–40.
3. In Genesee County, Michigan, for example, despite several flaws in the support enforcement program, the average noncustodial parent paid 87 percent of all child support due during the first six years of a support order, while only 15 percent of all noncustodial parents were ever jailed for nonpayment. By contrast, in Dane County, Wisconsin, where jailing was not used, only about one in five noncustodial parents paid as high as 87 percent during the same time period. By the sixth year of the support order, 71 percent of noncustodial parents in Dane but only 24 percent of those in Genesee paid nothing at all. See Chambers, pp. 75–78, 339.
4. See Chambers, pp. 201–11, 339.
5. See Chambers, pp. 223–24.
6. See Chambers, pp. 79–104.

8. Establishing Paternity

1. These are the blood tests currently available:

RED BLOOD CELL ANTIGEN TEST

This is the oldest type of blood test, the easiest to perform and the least expensive. It detects and classifies biochemicals bound to the surfaces of the red cells within the blood.

The test is performed by introducing into the blood sample certain antibodies that will cause certain known blood types to clump or clot. By observing which antibodies cause the blood to clot, the testers can determine what type of blood is in the sample. The basic blood types A, B, AB and O, and Rh negative or positive (plus several less well known classification systems) are determined by this method.

Because the red blood cell antigen test is inexpensive and easy to perform, it is generally used first. Since it is only 63 to 72 percent effective in proving paternity when used alone, however, it is usually followed by one of the other types of tests if it doesn't rule out the putative father and the case is still contested.

HUMAN LEUKOCYTE ANTIGENS (HLA) TEST

Leukocyte is the technical name for white blood cells, and HLAs are biochemicals bound to the surface of the white blood cells. Two different classes of HLAs (HLA-A and HLA-B) are used in paternity testing. Since a very large number of variations of both HLA-A and HLA-B occur in the general population (and none of the variations is very common), this test is extremely accurate.

The HLA test is performed by introducing into the blood sample certain antibodies known to kill blood cells containing each of the different HLA variations. The testers will be able to determine, based upon which antibodies kill the blood cells, which HLA variation is present in the blood.

This means that the blood sample must be handled quickly and carefully so the cells will still be alive when the tests are performed. For this reason, the test is more expensive than the others and may not be available in all locations.

This test, when used in combination with the inexpensive red blood cell test, will establish a 91 to 99 percent probability of paternity.

ELECTROPHORESIS (PROTEIN AND ENZYME ANALYSIS)

Electrophoresis is a test that measures and analyzes blood protein. Because individuals vary greatly in terms of the shape and electrical charges of blood proteins, this test is also quite accurate.

To conduct the test, technicians charge blood molecules with electricity and move them through a sort of gelatin. By observing the exact direction and distance of movement by the protein in the blood, they can determine the specific types of protein that are present.

Unlike HLA testing, electrophoresis does not require special handling to keep the blood cells alive before testing. It is therefore less expensive, and blood samples can be sent by mail if the test is not available locally.

This test, when used in combination with the inexpensive red blood cell test, establishes a 91 to 97 percent probability of paternity. If all three tests are used together, the probability is 99 percent or better.

Source: *A Guide for Judges in Child Support Enforcement,* U.S. Department of Health and Human Services (1983), pp. 43–49. Available free of charge from:

The National Child Support Enforcement Reference Center
6110 Executive Boulevard, Room 820
Rockville, Maryland 20852
(301) 443-5106

9. The Legal Process

1. Aspaklaria, Shelley, and Gerson Geltner, *Everything You Want to Know About Your Husband's Money . . . And Need to Know Before the Divorce* (New York: Thomas Y. Crowell, 1980), p. 190.
2. *Paternity Establishment Handbook,* U.S. Department of Health and Human Services (1981), p. 25. Available free of charge from:
   The National Child Support Enforcement Reference Center
   6110 Executive Boulevard, Room 820
   Rockville, Maryland 20852
   (301) 443-5106

10. Showing Your Family's Financial Needs

1. *USDA Estimates of the Cost of Raising a Child: A Guide to Their Use and Interpretation,* U.S. Department of Agriculture, Miscellaneous Publication No. 1411 (1981).
2. Bureau of the Census, U.S. Department of Commerce, *Child Support and Alimony: 1981* (Advance Report) Series P-23, No. 124, p. 2.
3. N. Hunter, "Child Support Law and Policy: The Systematic Imposition of Costs on Women," *Harvard Women's Law Journal* 6 (1983); and P. Eden, Forensic Economics—Use of Economists in Cases of Dissolution of Marriage, 17 *Am. Jur. Proof of Facts* 345 (2nd ed., 1978).
4. This method has been developed, using set formulas and government standard of living charts, by economist Phillip Eden and others. See note 3.

12. The Truth About Alimony

1. In 1981, only about 5 percent of divorced or separated (nonremarried) women actually received any alimony in that year. Of those that did, the mean amount received was a mere $3000 a year. Obviously unable to live on the alimony, about three-fourths of the alimony recipients worked outside the home in addition to their family and child-raising responsibilities. Those who didn't hold outside jobs lived not in luxury but in poverty, with a mean total household income of only $6,484. See *Child Support and Alimony: 1981* (Advance Report), U.S. Department of Commerce, Bureau of the Census, Special Studies, Series P-23, No. 124.
2. See L. Weitzman, "The Economic Consequences of Divorce: An Empirical Study of Property, Alimony and Child Support Awards," *Family Law Reporter* 8:037 (1982).
3. See note 1.
4. See note 1.

13. Child Custody

1. A 1983 survey of 517 mothers without legal custody showed that 71 of them, or 14 percent, paid child support. Unpublished study by Geoffrey L. Greif of University of Maryland.
2. "Joint Custody Arrangements and AFDC Eligibility," *Clearinghouse Review* 18 (May 1984).
3. A 1979 Harvard-based study found women still doing all or most of the household chores. Ninety percent of the women and 85 percent of the men reported the wife was the one who changed the diapers. And in 1980, advertising agency surveys found men still resistant to housework and wanting most in a wife "a good mother who would assume responsibility for the children." *New York Times,* April 3, 1979, and November 1, 1980. See also Robinson, John, *How Americans Use Time: A Social-Psychological Analysis* (New York: Holt, Rinehart & Winston, Praeger Books, 1977).
4. In a study of Los Angeles County court statistics, researchers found that fathers received custody in only 5 to 6 percent of all divorce cases involving children, but that their success rate in gaining custody when they requested it was an impressive 63 percent. See Weitzman and Dixon, "Child Custody Awards: Legal Standards and Empirical Patterns for Child Custody, Support and Visitation After Divorce," 12 *U.C.D. Law Review* 471, 502–04 (1979). A study of Minneapolis courts found fathers winning in 45 percent of disputed cases. M. Wheeler, *Divided Children: A Legal Guide for Divorcing Parents* 40 (1980). In North Carolina, a survey of judges also showed fathers prevailing in nearly half of all custody disputes. Orthner and Lewis, "Evidence of Single Father Competence in Child Rearing" 13 *Fam. L.Q.* 27, 28 (1979).
5. For more historical background as well as a case-by-case analysis of the recent trends discussed in this section, see Polikoff, "Why Mothers are Losing: A Brief Analysis of Criteria Used in Child Custody Determinations," 7 *Women's Rights Law Reporter* 235 (1982). Also available from the NCWFL, note 3 ($1.20 each).
6. See Foster and Freed, "Divorce in the Fifty States: An Overview," 14 *Family L.Q.* 229 (1981).
7. See, e.g., *Michigan Comp. Laws Ann.* 722.23(c).
8. For an excellent and detailed analysis of recent joint custody legislation, see Schulman, "Who's Looking After the Children?" *Family Advocate* 5 (1982): 31. Reprints available from the National Center on Women and Family Law (NCWFL), 799 Broadway, Room 402, New York, New York 10003 ($1.50 each).
9. See, e.g., *Garska v. McCoy*, 278 S.E.2d 357 (W. Va. 1981), and *Jordan v. Jordan*, 8 *Fam. L. Rep.* (BNA) 2596 (Pa. 1982).

14. Keeping Your Family Safe

1. Report of the National League of Cities and the U.S. Conference of Mayors, cited in R. Langley and R. Levy, *Wife-Beating: The Silent Crisis* (New York: E.P. Dutton, 1977), p. 11.

2. J. Herman, *Father-Daughter Incest* (Cambridge, Mass.: Harvard University Press, 1981), pp. 7–21.

3. Because child support collection efforts can endanger formerly battered women and their children, they should never be required where there is a history or danger of violence or abuse. The Office of Child Support Enforcement, which ordinarily requires any woman receiving AFDC to cooperate in collection efforts, must make an exception whenever good cause to do so is shown. "Good cause" includes potential physical harm to mother or child, potential emotional harm to the child or potential emotional harm to the mother sufficient to interfere with her child-raising abilities.

4. Report of Police Foundation and National Institute of Justice, conducted in cooperation with Minneapolis Police Department, 1981–82. Available from:
Police Foundation
1909 K Street, N.W.
Suite 400
Washington, D.C. 20006

5. L. Walker, *The Battered Woman Syndrome* (New York: Springer Publishing Company, 1984).

6. From the Al-Anon Suggested Closing.

Resources

FREE INFORMATION ON CHILD SUPPORT

The best source of free information on child support is the National Child Support Enforcement Reference Center, 6110 Executive Boulevard, Rockville, Maryland 20852; (301) 443-5106. Among the available materials are:

Child Support Report. A monthly newsletter of new developments in support enforcement in the Office of Child Support Enforcement.

Two publications helpful for enforcement groups working to improve state laws: *State Statutes and the 1984 Federal Child Support Amendments* and *Selected Exemplary State Child Support Laws.*

Child Support: An Annotated Legal Bibliography. A complete listing of books and articles on child support.

A free handbook describing the services of the Office of Child Support Enforcement is also available. Send a postcard or letter to Consumer Information Center, Dept. 43, Pueblo, Colorado 81009, requesting the *Handbook on Child Support Enforcement.*

BOOKS ON RELATED TOPICS

The Divorce Handbook, by James T. Friedman (New York: Random House, 1982). A clear, comprehensive consumer's guide to the divorce process, written in question-and-answer format.

The Custody Handbook: A Woman's Guide to Child Custody Disputes, by Nancy Polikoff (1984). This important book is essential for any woman facing a possible custody conflict or considering a custody decision. It's available for $4 from the Women's Legal Defense Fund, 2000 P Street, N.W., Suite 400, Washington, D.C. 20036.

179

Everything You Want to Know About Your Husband's Money . . . And Need to Know Before the Divorce, by Shelley Aspaklaria and Gerson Geltner (New York: Crowell, 1980). Despite the awful title, this is an extremely helpful guide to divorce finances. Skip over the chapter called "The Tax Man," though, because recent tax law changes have made it no longer accurate.

The Single Mother's Handbook, by Elizabeth Greywolf (New York: William Morrow Press, 1984). A practical guide to coping with children, money, time and work.

Getting Free: A Handbook for Women in Abusive Relationships, by Ginny NiCarthy (Seattle: Seale Press, 1982). A helpful handbook of laws and services that can help you protect yourself against a violent partner, plus practical and personal considerations.

The Divorce Revolution, by Lenore Weitzman (New York: The Free Press, 1985). An excellent examination of the problems created by such recent divorce trends as no-fault divorce, changing custody standards and mediation. Not primarily a how-to book, but helpful for understanding the problem.

Making Fathers Pay: The Enforcement of Child Support, by David Chambers (University of Chicago Press: 1979). Not a how-to guide but very interesting reading about the advantages and disadvantages of using jailing to enforce support.

NATIONAL ORGANIZATIONS

Each of the listed organizations advocates improved child support enforcement as part of their program and goals. For membership or other information, contact the organization.

Parents Without Partners
7910 Woodmont Avenue, Suite 1000
Bethesda, MD 20814
(Single parent issues; newsletter and magazine)

The Children's Foundation
815 15th Street N.W., Suite 928
Washington, D.C. 20005
(Day care and child support advocacy; quarterly newsletter)

Children's Defense Fund
122 C Street N.W., Suite 400

Washington, D.C. 20001
(Children's legal rights; newsletter)

National Center on Women and Family Law
799 Broadway, Room 402
New York, New York 10003
(Women's and children's rights; child support information packets, newsletter)

Women's Legal Defense Fund
2000 P Street N.W., Suite 400
Washington, D.C. 20036
(Women's legal rights; newsletter)

The National Organization for Women (NOW)
1401 New York Avenue N.W., Suite 800
Washington, D.C. 20005
(Women's rights, education and advancement; newsletter)

National Women's Law Center
1616 P Street, N.W.
Washington, D.C. 20036
(Legislative and policy analysis, monitoring of OCSE compliance with law)

STATE ORGANIZATIONS

ALABAMA

State OCSE Agency
Paul Vincent, Director
Bureau of Child Support
Dept. of Pensions & Security
64 North Union Street
Montgomery, AL 36130
Telephone: 205/261-2872

URESA Information Agent
Paul Vincent, Director
Bureau of Child Support
Dept. of Pensions & Security
64 North Union Street
Montgomery, AL 36130
Telephone: 205/261-2872

URESA Interstate Inquiries and Complaints
Paul Vincent, Director
Bureau of Child Support
Dept. of Pensions & Security
64 North Union Street
Montgomery, AL 36130
Telephone: 205/261-2872

Parents' Support Enforcement Group
Kids in Need Deserve Equal Rights
(KINDER)
337 East Haven Drive
Birmingham, AL 35215
Contact: Judy Jennings 205/251-2223 (day)

ALASKA

State OCSE Agency
Dan Copeland, Director
Child Support Enforcement Agency
Department of Revenue
201 E. 9th Avenue, #202
Anchorage, AK 99501
Telephone: 907/276-3441

URESA Information Agent
Fred D. Smith,
  Chief Enforcement Officer
Child Support Enforcement Agency
Department of Revenue
201 E. 9th Avenue, #202, MS 01
Anchorage, AK 99501
Telephone: 907/276-3441, Ex. 266

AMERICAN SAMOA

Local OCSE Agency
URESA Information Agent
Asaua Fuimaono
Assistant Attorney General
Office of the Attorney General
P.O. Box 7
Pago Pago, American Samoa 96799
Telephone: 633-4163

ARIZONA

State OCSE Agency
John Ahl, Program Administrator
Child Support Enf. Administration
Dept. of Economic Security
P. O. Box 6123, Site Code 966C
Phoenix, AZ 85005
Telephone: 602/255-3465

URESA Information Agent
Hon. Robert Corbin
Arizona Attorney General
P.O. Box 6123, Site Code 775C
Phoenix, AZ 85005
Telephone: 602/255-5556

URESA Interstate Inquiries and Complaints
John Ahl, Program Administrator
Child Support Enf. Section
Dept. of Economic Security
P.O. Box 6123, Site Code 966C
Phoenix, AZ 85005
Telephone: 602/255-3465

Parents' Support Enforcement Group
Organization for Protection of America's Children
   (OPAC)
P.O. Box 1907
Scottsdale, AZ 85252
Contact: Terry Raetz 602/949-9803 (eve)
Kathy Browne 602/938-7206 (eve)

ARKANSAS

State OCSE Agency
Ed Baskin, Director
Office of Child Support Enforcement
Arkansas Social Services Division
P.O. Box 3358
Little Rock, AR 72203
Telephone: 501/371-2464

URESA Information Agent
Ivan H. Smith

Director of Legal Services
Arkansas Social Services Division
P.O. Box 1437
Little Rock, AR 72203
Telephone: 501/371-1981

URESA Interstate Inquiries and Complaints
Ivan H. Smith
Director of Legal Services
Arkansas Social Services Division
P.O. Box 1437
Little Rock, AR 72203
Telephone: 501/371-1981

CALIFORNIA

State OCSE Agency
Robert A. Barton, Chief
Child Support Program Management Branch
Department of Social Services
744 P Street
Sacramento, CA 95814
Telephone: 916/323-8994

URESA Information Agent
Gloria F. DeHart
Deputy Attorney General
Office of the Attorney General
6000 State Building
San Francisco, CA 94102
Telephone: 415/557-0799

URESA Interstate Inquiries and Complaints
Gloria F. DeHart
Deputy Attorney General
Office of the Attorney General
6000 State Building
San Francisco, CA 94102
Telephone: 415/557-0799

Parents' Support Enforcement Groups
Parents Organization for Support Enforcement
(POSE)
5212 Fairfax Road
Bakersfield, CA 93306
Contact: Charlie Wells 805/872-2985 (eve)

Single Parent Action Network
10560 Colona Road
Rancho Cordova, CA 95670
Contact: Mary Drummond 916/635-9176 (eve)

Single Parents United 'N' Kids
    (SPUNK)
5823 Marita Street
Long Beach, CA 90815
Contact: Susan Speir 213/598-9206 (eve)

Top Priority—Children
P.O. Box 2161
Palm Springs, CA 92263
Contact: Teddy Kieley 619/323-1559 (eve)

COLORADO

State OCSE Agency
    James Galeotti, Chief
    Child Support Enforcement Section
    Dept. of Social Services
    1575 Sherman St.
    Denver, CO 80203
    Telephone: 303/866-2422

URESA Information Agent
    Kenneth A. Switzer
    Child Support Enforcement Section
    Dept. of Social Services
    1575 Sherman St.
    Denver, CO 80203
    Telephone: 303/866-2422

URESA Interstate Inquiries and Complaints
    James Galeotti, Chief
    Child Support Enforcement Section
    Dept. of Social Services
    1575 Sherman St.
    Denver, CO 80203
    Telephone: 303/866-2422

Parents' Support Enforcement Group
    Kids in Need Deserve Equal Rights
        (KINDER)

5420 Wild Lane
Loveland, CO 80537
Contact: Mary Alice Chaffin 303/663-0949 (eve)

CONNECTICUT

State OCSE Agency
Anthony DiNallo, Chief
Div. of Child Support Enforcement
Dept. of Human Resources
110 Bartholomew Ave.
Hartford, CT 06115
Telephone: 203/566-3053

URESA Information Agent
A. J. Salius, Director
Superior Court, Family Division
28 Grand St.
Hartford, CT 06106
Telephone: 203/566-8187

URESA Interstate Inquiries and Complaints
A. J. Salius, Director
Superior Court, Family Division
28 Grand St.
Hartford, CT 06106
Telephone: 203/566-8187

Parents' Support Enforcement Groups
Parents Enforcing Court Ordered Support (PECOS)
25 Indian Run
Enfield, CT 06082
Contact: Patricia Caputo 203/749-0894

DELAWARE

State OCSE Agency
Frank F. Hindman, Acting Chief
Bur. of Child Support Enf.
Dept. of Health & Social Svcs.
P.O. Box 904
New Castle, DE 19720
Telephone: 302/571-3620

URESA Information Agent
Susan F. Paikin

Director of Support
Family Court of Delaware
900 King St., P.O. Box 2359
Wilmington, DE 19899
Telephone: 302/571-3867

URESA Interstate Inquiries and Complaints
Susan F. Paikin
Director of Support
Family Court of Delaware
900 King St., P.O. Box 2359
Wilmington, DE 19899
Telephone: 302/571-3867

DISTRICT OF COLUMBIA

Local OCSE Agency
Luis Rumbaut, Acting Chief
Bureau of Paternity/Child Support Enforcement
Dept. of Human Services
435 Eye Street, N.W.
Washington, DC 20001
Telephone: 202/727-8820

URESA Information Agent
Hugh O. Stevenson
Assistant Corporation Counsel
D.C. Office of Corporation Counsel
500 Indiana Ave. N.W., Rm. 4450
Washington, DC 20001
Telephone: 202/727-3839

URESA Interstate Inquiries and Complaints
Annette Simpson, URESA Coordinator
Bureau of Paternity/Child Sup. Enforcement
Dept. of Human Services
435 Eye St. N.W.
Washington, D.C. 20001
Telephone: 202/727-5058

FLORIDA

State OCSE Agency
Samuel G. Ashdown, Jr., Director
Child Support Enforcement
Dept. of Health & Rehabilitation Services

1317 Winewood Blvd.
Tallahassee, FL 32301
Telephone: 904/488-9900

URESA Information Agent
Samuel G. Ashdown, Jr., Director
Child Support Enforcement
Dept. of Health & Rehabilitation Services
1317 Winewood Blvd.
Tallahassee, FL 32301
Telephone: 904/488-9900

URESA Interstate Inquiries and Complaints
Samuel G. Ashdown, Jr.
URESA Information Agent
Office of Child Support Enf.
1317 Winewood Blvd.
Tallahassee, FL 32301
Telephone: 904/488-9900

Parents' Support Enforcement Groups
Children Against Deadbeat Dads (CADD)
P.O. Box 2010 E.V.
Ormand Beach, FL 32074
Contact: Marj Van Brackle
904/672-3499 (eve)

GEORGIA

State OCSE Agency
Jerry Townsend, Director
Office of Child Support Recovery
Dept. of Human Resources
878 Peachtree St., N.E., Box 80000
Atlanta, GA 30357
Telephone: 404/894-5087

URESA Information Agent
Spencer Lawton, Sr., Manager
Office of Child Support Recovery
Dept. of Human Resources
878 Peachtree St. NE, Box 80000
Atlanta, GA 30357
Telephone: 404/894-5933

URESA Interstate Inquiries and Complaints
Jerry Townsend, Director
Office of Child Support Recovery
Dept. of Human Resources
878 Peachtree St. NE, Box 80000
Atlanta, GA 30357
Telephone: 404/894-5087

Parents' Support Enforcement Groups
Coalition to Help Enforce Child Support
437 The North Chase
Atlanta, GA 30328
Contact: Arlene Gelbert (mail only)

GUAM

Local OCSE Agency
Julia Perez, Program Coordinator IV
Child Support Enforcement Office
Dept. of Public Health and Social Services
P.O. Box 2816
Agana, Guam 96910
Telephone: 671/734-2947

URESA Information Agent
Office of Attorney General
Department of Law
PDN Building, Suite 701
238 O'Hara St.
Agana, Guam 96910
Telephone: 671/462-6841

HAWAII

State OCSE Agency
James O'Brien, IV-D Director
Child Support Enforcement Agency
770 Kapiolani, #606
Honolulu, HI 96813
Telephone: 808/548-5779

URESA Information Agent
James O'Brien, IV-D Director
Child Support Enforcement Agency
770 Kapiolani, #606

Honolulu, HI 96813
Telephone: 808/548-5779

URESA Interstate Inquiries and Complaints
Catherine J. Carman
Child Support Enforcement Specialist V
Child Support Enforcement IV-D Agency
770 Kapiolani Blvd., Suite 606
Honolulu, HI 96813
Telephone: 808/548-6723

IDAHO

State OCSE Agency
Patricia Barrell, Chief
Bureau of Support Enforcement
Dept. of Health & Welfare
Statehouse Mail
Boise, ID 83720
Telephone: 208/334-4422

URESA Information Agent
Susan Peterson
Bureau of Support Enforcement
Dept. of Health & Welfare
Statehouse Mail
Boise, ID 83720
Telephone: 208/334-4418

URESA Interstate Inquiries and Complaints
Susan Peterson
Bureau of Support Enforcement
Dept. of Health & Welfare
Statehouse Mail
Boise, ID 83720
Telephone: 208/334-4418

ILLINOIS

State OCSE Agency
Gerald D. Slavens, Chief
Bureau of Child Support
Dept. of Public Aid
316 S. 2nd St.
Springfield, IL 62762
Telephone: 217/782-1366

URESA Information Agent
Gerald D. Slavens, Chief
Bureau of Child Support
Dept. of Public Aid
316 S. 2nd St.
Springfield, IL 62762
Telephone: 217/782-1366

URESA Interstate Inquiries and Complaints
Bureau of Child Support
Reciprocal Unit
225 S. 4th St.
P.O. Box 2127
Springfield, IL 62705
Telephone: 217/782-1388

INDIANA

State OCSE Agency
Paula Eggermann, Acting Director
Child Support Enf. Division
Dept. of Public Welfare
141 S. Meridian St., 4th Flr.
Indianapolis, IN 46225
Telephone: 317/232-4885

URESA Information Agent
URESA Coordinator
Child Support Enf. Division
Dept. of Public Welfare
141 S. Meridian St., 4th Flr.
Indianapolis, IN 46225
Telephone: 317/232-4906

URESA Interstate Inquiries and Complaints
Paula Eggermann, Acting Director
Child Support Enf. Division
Dept. of Public Welfare
141 S. Meridian St., 4th Flr.
Indianapolis, IN 46225
Telephone: 317/232-4885

Parents' Support Enforcement Group
Equal Rights for Children
181 Neringa Lane

Hobart, IN 46342
Contact: Cynthia Robbins 219/942-9973 (eve)

IOWA

State OCSE Agency
Christy Ill, Director
Child Support Recovery Unit
Dept. of Social Services
Hoover Building
Des Moines, IA 50319
Telephone: 515/281-5580

URESA Information Agent
Christy Ill, Director
Child Support Recovery Unit
Dept. of Social Services
Hoover Building
Des Moines, IA 50319
Telephone: 515/281-5580

URESA Interstate Inquiries and Complaints
Christy Ill, Director
Child Support Recovery Unit
Dept. of Social Services
Hoover Building
Des Moines, IA 50319
Telephone: 515/281-5580

KANSAS

State OCSE Agency
Donald L. Bears, Administrator
Child Support Enforcement Program
Dept. of Social & Rehabilitation Services
Perry Building, 2700 W. 6th
Topeka, KS 66606
Telephone: 913/296-3237

URESA Information Agent
Senior Legal Counsel
Child Support Enforcement Program
Dept. of Social & Rehabilitation Services
Perry Building, 2700 W. 6th
Topeka, KS 66606
Telephone: 913/296-3237

KENTUCKY

State OCSE Agency
Hanson Williams, Director
Div. for Child Support Enforcement
Cabinet for Human Resources
275 E. Main St., 6 Flr. E.
Frankfort, KY 40621
Telephone: 502/564-2285

URESA Information Agent
David E. Cathers, Staff Attorney
Office of the Counsel
Cabinet for Human Resources
275 E. Main St., 4 Flr. W.
Frankfort, KY 40621
Telephone: 502/564-7900

URESA Interstate Inquiries and Complaints
Steven P. Veno
Contracts Operation Section Spvsr.
Cabinet for Human Resources
275 E. Main St., 6 Flr. W.
Frankfort, KY 40621
Telephone: 502/564-2285

Parents' Support Enforcement Group
Mothers for Child Support
Rte. 1 Box 358
Rineyville, KY 40162
Contact: Vicki Gaddie 502/765-5733

LOUISIANA

State OCSE Agency
Marjorie T. Stewart, Asst. Sec.
Support Enforcement Services
Dept. of Health & Human Resources
P.O. Box 44276
Baton Rouge, LA 70804
Attn: P. M. Blakney
Telephone: 504/342-4780

URESA Information Agent
Marjorie T. Stewart, Asst. Sec.
Support Enforcement Services

Dept. of Health & Human Resources
P.O. Box 44276
Baton Rouge, LA 70804
Attn: Perry MacPee
Telephone: 504/342-4780

URESA Interstate Inquiries and Complaints
Marjorie T. Stewart, Asst. Sec.
Support Enforcement Services
Dept. of Health & Human Resources
P.O. Box 44276
Baton Rouge, LA 70804
Attn: P. M. Blakney
Telephone: 504/342-4780

Parents' Support Enforcement Groups
Kids in Need Deserve Equal Rights
(KINDER)
P. O. Box 6225
Shreveport, LA 71136
Contact: Deborah Dean 318/747-0346 (eve)

Support Your Children
P. O. Box 80836
Baton Rouge, LA 70898
Contact: Jane Crawford 504/388-6624 (day)

MAINE

State OCSE Agency
Colburn W. Jackson, Director
Support Enforcement Program
Department of Human Services
State House, Station 11
Augusta, ME 04333
Telephone: 207/289-2886

URESA Information Agent
Colburn W. Jackson, Director
Support Enforcement Program
Department of Human Services
State House, Station 11
Augusta, ME 04333
Telephone: 207/289-2886

MARYLAND

State OCSE Agency
Ann C. Helton, Executive Director
Child Support Enforcement Admin.
Dept. of Human Resources
300 W. Preston St.
Baltimore, MD 21201
Telephone: 301/576-5388

URESA Information Agent
John M. Williams
State Information Agent
DHR/Child Support Enf. Admin.
300 W. Preston St., Rm. 502
Baltimore, MD 21201
Telephone: 301/576-5498

URESA Interstate Inquiries and Complaints
John M. Williams
State Information Agent
DHR/Child Support Enforcement Admin.
300 W. Preston St., Rm. 502
Baltimore, MD 21201
Telephone: 301/576-5498

Parents' Support Enforcement Groups
Mothers United for Support Enforcement
3711 37th Avenue
Cottage City, MD 20722
Contact: Anna Angolia 301/779-3999 (eve)
Rosalind Johnson 301/773-0976 (eve)

Organization for the Enforcement of Child Support (OECS)
119 Nicodemus Road
Reistertown, MD 21136
Contact: Elaine and William Fromm 301/833-2458 (eve)

MASSACHUSETTS

State OCSE Agency
Fred Brown, Director
Child Support Enforcement Unit
Department of Public Welfare

600 Washington St.
Boston, MA 02111
Telephone: 617/727-7820

URESA Information Agent
Fred Brown, Director
Child Support Enforcement Unit
Department of Public Welfare
600 Washington St.
Boston, MA 02111
Telephone: 617/727-7820

Parents' Support Enforcement Groups
Massachusetts Child Support Payment Friends
P. O. Box 142
Charlton Depot, MA 01509
Contact: Donna Bigelow 617/248-5271 (eve)

Mothers United to Save the Children Through Legislative Efforts
(MUSCLE)
P.O. Box 176
Williamsburg, MA 01096
Contact: Cindy Foster 413/268-7028 (eve)

MICHIGAN

State OCSE Agency
Jerrold H. Brockmyre, Director
Office of Child Support
Department of Social Services
300 S. Capitol Ave., Box 30037
Lansing, MI 48909
Telephone: 517/373-7570

URESA Information Agent
Jerrold H. Brockmyre, Director
Office of Child Support
Department of Social Services
300 S. Capitol Ave., Box 30037
Lansing, MI 48909
Attn: URESA Coordinator
Telephone: 517/373-6782

URESA Interstate Inquiries and Complaints
URESA Coordinator

Office of Child Support
Department of Social Services
300 S. Capitol Ave., Box 30037
Lansing, MI 48909
Telephone: 517/373-7570

MINNESOTA

State OCSE Agency
Bonnie L. Becker, Director
Office of Child Support Enforcement
Department of Public Welfare
Space Center Building
444 Lafayette Rd.
St. Paul, MN 55101
Telephone: 612/296-2499

URESA Information Agent
Bonnie L. Becker, Director
Office of Child Support Enforcement
Department of Public Welfare
Space Center Bldg.
444 Lafayette Rd.
St. Paul, MN 55101
Telephone: 612/296-2499

URESA Interstate Inquiries and Complaints
Mary L. Anderson, Program Adviser
Office of Child Support Enforcement
Department of Public Welfare
Space Center Bldg., 2nd Flr.
444 Lafayette Road
St. Paul, MN 55101
612/296-2555

MISSISSIPPI

State OCSE Agency
Monte L. Barton, Director
Child Support Division
Dept. of Public Welfare
515 E. Amite St., Box 352
Jackson, MS 39205
Telephone: 601/354-0341, Ex. 503

URESA Information Agent
Oscar Mackey
Assistant Attorney General
Mississippi Attorney General
P. O. Box 220
Jackson, MS 39205
Telephone: 601/354-7130

URESA Interstate Inquiries and Complaints
Director, Child Support Dept.
Dept. of Public Welfare
P.O. Box 352
Jackson, MS 39205
Telephone: 601/354-0341, Ex. 502

MISSOURI

State OCSE Agency
Paul R. Nelson, Administrator
Child Support Enforcement Unit
Division of Family Service
911 Missouri Blvd., Box 88
Jefferson City, MO 65103
Telephone: 314/751-4301

URESA Information Agent
Child Support Enforcement Unit
Division of Family Service
911 Missouri Blvd., Box 88
Jefferson City, MO 65103
Telephone: 314/751-4301

URESA Interstate Inquiries and Complaints
Paul R. Nelson, Administrator
Child Support Enforcement Unit
Division of Family Service
911 Missouri Blvd., Box 88
Jefferson City, MO 65103
Telephone: 314/751-4301

Parents' Support Enforcement Groups
Organization for Child Support Action (OCSA)
P. O. Box 188
High Ridge, MO 63049
Contact: Beverly Bohmie 314/677-8911

Parents United for Lawful Support Enforcement (PULSE)
12 Parkview Drive
St. Peters, MO 63376
Contact: Betty Murphy 314/279-1441 (eve)

MONTANA

State OCSE Agency
William Harrington, Chief
Inves. and Enforcement Bureau
Department of Revenue
P.O. Box 5955
Helena, MT 59604
Telephone: 406/449-4614

URESA Information Agent
William Harrington, Chief
Inves. and Enforcement Bureau
Department of Revenue
P.O. Box 5955
Helena, MT 59604
Telephone: 406/449-4614

URESA Interstate Inquiries and Complaints
Dennis Shober, Program Manager
Child Support Enforcement Program
Department of Revenue
1410 1.2 8th Ave.
Helena, MT 59620
Telephone: 406/444-3347

NEBRASKA

State OCSE Agency
Robert Huston, Administrator
Child Support Enforcement Office
Department of Social Services
301 Centennial Mall S., 5 Flr.
Box 95026
Lincoln, NE 68509

URESA Information Agent
Gina C. Dunning, Director
Department of Social Services
301 Centennial Mall S., 5 Flr.

Box 95026
Lincoln, NE 68509
Telephone: 402/471-3121

URESA Interstate Inquiries and Complaints
Gina C. Dunning, Director
Department of Social Services
301 Centennial Mall S.,
 5 Flr.
Box 95026
Lincoln, NE 68509
Telephone: 402/471-3121

Parents' Support Enforcement Group
Child Support Task Force
1514 N. 76th St.
Omaha, NE 68114
Contact: Kathy Schultz
Telephone: 402/397-3284 (eve)

NEVADA

State OCSE Agency
William F. Furlong
Child Support Enforcement
Nevada State Welfare Division
251 Jeanell Drive
Carson City, NV 89710
Telephone: 702/885-4744

URESA Information Agent
Brian McKay, Attorney General
Office of Attorney General
Hero's Memorial Building
Capitol Complex
Carson City, NV 89710
Telephone: 702/885-4170

URESA Interstate Inquiries and Complaints
William F. Furlong
Child Support Enforcement
Nevada State Welfare Division
251 Jeanell Drive
Carson City, NV 89710
Telephone: 702/885-4744

NEW HAMPSHIRE

State OCSE Agency
Arthur A. Stukas, Admin.
Ofc. of Child Support Enforcement Services
Division of Welfare
Health & Welfare Building, Hazen Dr.
Concord, NH 03301
Telephone: 603/271-4426

URESA Information Agent
Interstate Coordination/URESA Cont.
Ofc. of Child Support Enforcement Services
Division of Welfare
Health & Welfare Bldg., Hazen Dr.
Concord, NH 03301
Telephone: 603/271-4427

NEW JERSEY

State OCSE Agency
Harry W. Wiggins, Chief
Bureau of Child Support & Paternity Programs
Department of Human Services
C.N. 716
Trenton, NJ 08625
Telephone: 609/633-6268

URESA Information Agent
Robert D. Lipscher, Administrative Director
Administrative Office of the Courts
C.N. 037
Trenton, NJ 08625
Telephone: 609/292-1087

URESA Interstate Inquiries and Complaints
Harry W. Wiggins, Chief
Bureau of Child Support & Paternity Programs
Department of Human Services
C.N. 716
Trenton, NJ 08625
Telephone: 609/633-6268

Parents' Support Enforcement Groups
Organization for Child Support Action

P.O. Box 1401
Burlington, NJ 08016
Contact: Judi Richter 609/386-6211 (eve)

Organization for the Enforcement of Child Support (OECS)
P.O. Box 5227
Parsippany, NJ 07054
Contact: Janet Saulter-Hemmer 201/334-0281 (eve)

NEW MEXICO

State OCSE Agency
Ben Silva, Chief
Child Support Enforcement Bureau
Department of Human Services
P.O. Box 2348, PERA Bldg.
Santa Fe, NM 87503
Telephone: 505/827-5591

URESA Information Agent
Carliss Thalley
Legal Services Bureau
Department of Human Services
P.O. Box 2348
Santa Fe, NM 87503
Telephone: 505/827-2305

NEW YORK

State OCSE Agency
Meldon F. Kelsey, Director
Office of Child Support Enforcement
P.O. Box 14
One Commerce Plaza
Albany, NY 12260
Telephone: 518/474-9081

URESA Information Agent
Joseph E. Bissell, Esq.
Interstate Legal Unit
Office of Child Support Enforcement
P.O. Box 14, One Commerce Plaza
Albany, NY 12260
Telephone: 518/473-0929

URESA Interstate Inquiries and Complaints
Joseph E. Bissell, Esq.
Interstate Legal Unit
Office of Child Support Enforcement
P.O. Box 14, One Commerce Plaza
Albany, NY 12260
Telephone: 518/473-0929

Parents' Support Enforcement Groups
For Our Children and Us (FOCUS)
550 Old Country Road
Hicksville, NY 11801
Contact: Fran Mattera 516/433-6633

Separated Persons Living in Transition (SPLIT)
1805 Fifth Avenue
North Bay Shore, NY 11706
Contact: Virginia Engle 516/435-0740

NORTH CAROLINA

State OCSE Agency
Susan C. Smith, Chief
Child Support Enforcement Section
Division of Social Services
Department of Human Resources
443 N. Harrington St.
Raleigh, NC 27603-1393
Telephone: 919/733-4120

URESA Information Agent
John Syria, Director
Division of Social Services
Department of Human Resources
443 N. Harrington St.
Raleigh, NC 27603-1393
Attn: Kathy Futrell
Telephone: 919/733-4120

URESA Interstate Inquiries and Complaints
Kathy L. Futrell
Interstate/URESA Coordinator
Child Support Enforcement Section
441-443 N. Harrington St.

Raleigh, NC 27603
Telephone: 919/733-4120

NORTH DAKOTA

State OCSE Agency
Marcellus Hartze, Administrator
Child Support Enforcement Agency
Social Service Board of North Dakota
State Capitol
Bismarck, ND 58505
Telephone: 701/224-3582

URESA Information Agent
Marcellus Hartze, Administrator
Child Support Enforcement Agency
Social Service Board of North Dakota
State Capitol
Bismarck, ND 58505
Telephone: 701/224-3582

URESA Interstate Inquiries and Complaints
Marcellus Hartze, Administrator
Child Support Enforcement Agency
Social Service Board of North Dakota
State Capitol
Bismarck, ND 58505
Telephone: 701/224-3582

OHIO

State OCSE Agency
Chief
Bureau of Child Support
Department of Public Welfare
State Office Tower
30 Broad Street East, 31st Floor
Columbus, OH 43215
Telephone: 614/466-3233

URESA Information Agent
Chief, State Departments Section
Office of Attorney General
State Office Tower
30 Broad Street East, 16th Floor

Columbus, OH 43215
Telephone: 614/466-8600

Parents' Support Enforcement Groups
Association for Children for Enforcement of Support
(ACES)
1018 Jefferson Avenue #204
Toledo, OH 43624
Contact: Geraldine Jensen 419/242-6129 (eve)

Legal Advocacy for Women (LAW)
410 Bennett Street
Bridgeport, OH 43912
Contact: Pat Wilson 614/676-2042

Non-Support, Inc.
544 Milan
Canal Fulton, OH 44614
Contact: Sandie Sterns 216/644-0061

OKLAHOMA

State OCSE Agency
Wesley Rucker, IV-D Administrator
Attn: Division of Child Support
Department of Human Services
P.O. Box 25352
Oklahoma City, OK 73125
Telephone: 405/424-5871

URESA Information Agent
Wesley Rucker, IV-D Administrator
Attn: Division of Child Support
Department of Human Services
P.O. Box 25352
Oklahoma City, OK 73125
Telephone: 405/424-5871

URESA Interstate Inquiries and Complaints
Robert Fulton, Director
Department of Human Services
P.O. Box 25352
Oklahoma City, OK 73125
Attn: Programs Administrator

Child Support Enf. Unit
Telephone: 405/424-5871 Ext. 2642

Parents' Support Enforcement Groups
Support Our Children
P.O. Box 30888
Midwest City, OK 73140
Contact: Paula Brooks 405/391-4027 (mornings)

OREGON

State OCSE Agency
Leonard T. Sytsma, Manager
DHR/AFS Recovery Services Section
502 Public Service Building
P.O. Box 14506 (Zip 97309)
Salem, OR 97310
Telephone: 503/378-6429

URESA Information Agent
Jim Hunter, Administrator
Support Enforcement Division
Department of Justice
Justice Building
Salem, OR 97310
Telephone: 503/378-4879

URESA Interstate Inquiries and Complaints
Jim Hunter, Administrator
Support Enforcement Division
Department of Justice
Justice Building
Salem, OR 97310
Telephone: 503/378-4879

PENNSYLVANIA

State OCSE Agency
John F. Stuff, Director
Child Support Programs
Dept. of Public Welfare
P.O. Box 8018
Harrisburg, PA 17105
Telephone: 717/783-1779

URESA Information Agent
John F. Stuff, Director
Child Support Programs
Dept. of Public Welfare
P.O. Box 8018
Harrisburg, PA 17105
Telephone: 717/783-1779

URESA Interstate Inquiries and Complaints
Robert Barton, Manager
Parent Locator Services
Child Support Programs
P.O. Box 8018
Harrisburg, PA 17105

Parents' Support Enforcement Groups
Legal Advocacy for Women (LAW)
429 Forbes Avenue
Pittsburgh, PA 15219
Contact: Rosemary Palmer 412/255-6708 (day)
Monaca chapter: Melanie Summerville 412/728-0681 (eve)
Somerset chapter: Phyllis Mitchell 814/443-2532
814/536-5115

Support for Dependent Children
318 Garber Street
Holidaysburg, PA 16648
Contact: Millie McClain 814/695-5336

Women's Network
905 Atwood Road
Philadelphia, PA 19118
Contact: Leigh Fraser 215/646-1363

PUERTO RICO

Local OCSE Agency
Miguel A. Verdiales, Director
Child Support Enforcement Program
Department of Social Services
P.O. Box 11398
Fernandez Juncos Station
Santurce, PR 00910
Telephone: 809/722-4731

URESA Information Agent
  Ada E. Rivera-Sepulveda, Chief
  Reciprocal Support Division
  Office of Court Administration
  Hato Rey Station, Call Box 22A
  Hato Rey, PR 00919
  Telephone: 809/764-7145

RHODE ISLAND

State OCSE Agency
  George A. Moriarty
  Chief Supervisor
  Bureau of Family Support
  77 Dorrance Street
  Providence, RI 02903
  Telephone: 401/277-2409

URESA Information Agent
  George A. Moriarty
  Chief Supervisor
  Bureau of Family Support
  77 Dorrance Street
  Providence, RI 02903
  Telephone: 401/277-2409

URESA Interstate Inquiries and Complaints
  Paul Palmera
  Bureau of Family Support
  77 Dorrance Street
  Providence, RI 02903
  Telephone: 401/277-6933

SOUTH CAROLINA

State OCSE Agency
  Paul W. Chavious, Director
  Division of Child Support
  Department of Social Services
  P.O. Box 1520
  Columbia, SC 29202
  Telephone: 803/758-3151

URESA Information Agent
  Division of Child Support
  Department of Social Services

P.O. Box 1520
Columbia, SC 29202
Telephone: 803/758-8860

Parents' Support Enforcement Group
Organization for Child Support Action
(OCSA)
Route 9, Box 272
Wyatt Drive #10
Spartanburg, SC 29301
Contact: Felicia Richards 803/574-6347

SOUTH DAKOTA

State OCSE Agency
Terry Walter, Program Administrator
Office of Child Support Enforcement
700 N. Illinois St.
Pierre, SD 57501
Telephone: 605/773-3641

URESA Information Agent
Janice Godtland
Assistant Attorney General
Attorney General's Office
700 N. Illinois St.
Pierre, SD 57501
Telephone: 605/773-3305

TENNESSEE

State OCSE Agency
Joyce D. McClaran, Director
Office of Child Support Services
Department of Human Services
111–19 7th Avenue N., 5 Flr.
Nashville, TN 37203
Telephone: 615/741-1820

URESA Information Agent
Department of Human Services
111–19 7th Avenue N., 5 Flr.
Nashville, TN 37203
Telephone: 615/741-1939
Attn: Sue Ellis, Internal Coordinator
Office of Child Support Services

URESA Interstate Inquiries and Complaints
Sue Ellis, Interstate Coordinator
Department of Human Services
111–19 7th Avenue N., 5 Flr.
Nashville, TN 37203
Telephone: 615/741-1939

TEXAS

State OCSE Agency
Lewis J. Zegub, Assistant Commissioner
Child Support Enforcement Branch
Department of Human Resources
P.O. Box 2960
Austin, TX 78769
Telephone: 512/835-0440

URESA Information Agent
Child Support Enforcement Program
Office of the Attorney General
P.O. Box 12548
Austin, TX 78711-2548
Telephone: 512/475-0990

Parents' Support Enforcement Groups
Parents for Child Support Enforcement
2930 Healey
Dallas, TX 75228
Contact: Doraldine Barrera 214/824-1620 (day)
214/270-6058 (eve)

Parents for Kids
6913 Bal Lake Dr.
Fort Worth, TX 76116
Contact: Charlotte Boeker 817/451-0482 (eve)
Stella Cable 817/737-4115 (eve)

UTAH

State OCSE Agency
John P. Abbott, Director
Office of Recovery Services
Bureau of Child Support Enforcement
3195 S. Main St., Box 15400
Salt Lake City, UT 84115

URESA Information Agent
Bruce Black, Manager
URESA Coordination
3195 S. Main St., Box 15400
Salt Lake City, UT 84115
Telephone: 801/483-6274

URESA Interstate Inquiries and Complaints
Bruce Black, Manager
Locate Coordination
3195 S. Main St., Box 15400
Salt Lake City, UT 84115
Telephone: 801/483-6274

VERMONT

State OCSE Agency
William D. Kirby, Director
Child Support Division
Department of Social Welfare
103 S. Main St.
Waterbury, VT 05676
Telephone: 802/241-2868

URESA Information Agent
Joan B. Kilton, Paralegal
Child Support Division
Department of Social Welfare
103 S. Main St.
Waterbury, VT 05676
Telephone: 802/241-2846

URESA Interstate Inquiries and Complaints
Joan B. Kilton, Paralegal
Child Support Division
Department of Social Welfare
103 S. Main St.
Waterbury, VT 05676
Telephone: 802/241-2846

VIRGIN ISLANDS

Local OCSE Agency
Alden Martinez, Director
Paternity & Child Support Unit
Department of Law

P.O. Box 1074
Christiansted, St. Croix, VI 00820
Telephone: 809/773-8240

URESA Information Agent
Attorney General
Department of Law
P.O. Box 280, Charlotte Amalie
St. Thomas, VI 00801
Attn: URESA
Telephone: 809/774-5666

VIRGINIA

State OCSE Agency
Jean M. White, Director
Div. of Support Enforcement
Department of Social Services
8007 Discovery Drive
Richmond, VA 23288
Telephone: 804/281-9154

URESA Information Agent
Jean M. White, Director
Div. of Support Enforcement
Department of Social Services
8007 Discovery Drive
Richmond, VA 23288
Telephone: 804/281-9104

URESA Interstate Inquiries and Complaints
Jean M. White, Director
Div. of Support Enforcement
Department of Social Services
8007 Discovery Drive
Richmond, VA 23288
Telephone: 804/281-9154

Parents' Support Enforcement Groups
For Our Children's Unpaid Support
    (FOCUS)
P. O. Box 2183
Vienna, VA 22180
Contact: Bettianne Welsh 703/860-1123

Virginians Organized in the Interest of Children's Entitlement
to Support (VOICES)
P. O. Box 12060
Arlington, VA 22209
Contact: Linda Whittington 703/765-0492 (eve)
Northern Virginia: Lori Morelock 703/281-3614 (eve)
Richmond: Celia McGuckian 804/320-1871 (eve)

WASHINGTON

State OCSE Agency
Jon Conine, Acting Director
Office of Support Enforcement
Dept. of Social & Health Services
P.O. Box 9162-MS FU-11
Olympia, WA 98504
Telephone: 206/459-6481

URESA Information Agent
David R. Minikel
Assistant Attorney General
Dept. of Social & Health Services
Attorney General Division
PY-13
Olympia, WA 98504
Telephone: 206/459-6574

Parent Location Service
Carol Cole, SEO I
Locate Section
Office of Support Enforcement
Dept. of Social & Health Services
P.O. Box 9162-MS FU-11
Olympia, WA 98504
Telephone: 206/459-6454

Parents' Support Enforcement Group
Need for Support Enforcement
12638 SE 7th Place
Bellevue, WA 98005
Contact: Bea Kriloff 206/453-1941

WEST VIRGINIA

State OCSE Agency
Sandra K. Gilmore, Director

Office of Child Support Enforcement
Department of Human Services
1900 Washington St. East
Charleston, WV 25305
Telephone: 304/348-3780

URESA Information Agent
Cona H. Chatman, URESA Coordinator
Office of Child Support Enforcement
Department of Human Services
1900 Washington St. East
Charleston, WV 25305
Telephone: 304/348-3780

URESA Interstate Inquiries and Complaints
Cona H. Chatman
Office of Child Support Enforcement
Department of Human Services
1900 Washington St. East
Charleston, WV 25305
Telephone: 304/348-3780

Parents' Support Enforcement Group
Legal Advocacy for Women (LAW)
Rte. 2, Box 134C
New Martinsville, WV 26155
Contact: Ginnie Guthrie 304/758-4353

WISCONSIN

State OCSE Agency
Duane Campbell, Director
Office of Child Support
Division of Community Services
Dept. of Health & Social Services
Box 8913
Madison, WI 53708
Telephone: 608/266-0528

URESA Information Agent
Betty Massey, Specialist
Office of Child Support
Division of Community Services

Dept. of Health & Social Services
Box 8913
Madison, WI 53708
Telephone: 608/266-0252

WYOMING

State OCSE Agency
Shirley Kingston, Director
Child Support Enforcement Section
Dept. of Health & Social Services
Hathaway Building
Cheyenne, WY 82002
Telephone: 307/777-7561

URESA Information Agent
Laura Beard
Deputy Attorney General
Office of Attorney General
State Capitol Building
Cheyenne, WY 82002
Telephone: 307/777-7841

URESA Interstate Inquiries and Complaints
Shirley Kingston, Director
Child Support Enforcement Section
Dept. of Health & Social Services
Hathaway Building
Cheyenne, WY 82002
Telephone: 307/777-7561

Index

217

A Special Announcement for Child Support Enforcement Groups

Does your parents' enforcement group have a special project in need of extra funding? If so, you may be interested in this open grant opportunity. The author of this book has pledged to donate 10 percent of all post-publication royalties to parents' enforcement groups. Your group can apply any time after January 1, 1986.

Grants will be awarded based upon available funds, the goals and activities of the enforcement group, and the likelihood that the project will bring about positive social change. Education and outreach, legislative advocacy and local policy advocacy projects are all encouraged. Matching grants coordinated with local fund-raising efforts will be made whenever possible.

Initial grants will be small—perhaps $100.00 to $500.00—so that as many groups as possible can be reached. Repeat grants in subsequent years will be awarded if funds permit and the group has shown significant progress.

Grant proposals need not be overly formal, but they should give as much information as possible about:

- The membership of the group
- The specific goals of the group
- Past activities, successes and difficulties
- The specific project for which you are requesting a grant
- Other funding sources and fundraising plans

To submit a proposal, or for more information, contact:

Marianne Takas
40 Harper & Row, Publishers, Inc.
10 East 53rd Street
New York, NY 10022